GOD'S APPOINTED CUSTOMS

GOD'S APPOINTED CUSTOMS

A Messianic Jewish Guide to
the Biblical Lifecycle and Lifestyle

Barney Kasdan

MESSIANIC JEWISH PUBLISHERS
a division of
The Lederer Foundation
Baltimore, Maryland

04 03 02 01 00 99 98   8 7 6 5 4 3 2
ISBN 1–880226–63–4

Messianic Jewish Publishers,
a division of The Lederer Foundation
6204 Park Heights Avenue, Baltimore, MD 21215

410-358-6471
order line: 800-410-7367
e-mail: LedMessMin@aol.com
Internet: http://www.MessianicJewish.net

Table of Contents

Acknowledgements

My thanks go to several people who were a part of the process of this book. Members of *Kehilat Ariel* Messianic Congregation of San Diego helped formulate some of the ideas presented in this book. In addition, Bryan Zaremsky provided graphics that help one to visualize many of the Jewish customs.

I wish to give special honor to my parents, Shelley and Norma Kasdan, who have always provided encouragement and support. Since 1971, we have been unified in the faith of Yeshua ("Jesus") the Messiah, for which I give eternal thanks. My wife, Liz Kasdan, deserves special recognition as my *eshet chayil*, "wife of valor" (Proverbs 31:10), and loving partner. Our four beautiful kids (David, Aaron, Zhava and Dvora) have been a blessing as we have developed our Messianic Jewish lifestyle. Finally, thanksgiving and praise go to the God of Israel and my redeemer, *Yeshua HaMashiakh*, for his indescribable gift (2 Corinthians 9:15).

Introduction

THE IMPORTANCE OF CUSTOMS

Tradition!

While the song and concept were popularized by Tevye in *Fiddler On the Roof*, tradition is something that has been with the Jewish people for several millennia. The Hebrew Scriptures have long been the foundation of Jewish life and practice. Yet, as immense as the Bible is, many details need explaining. Welcome to the world of tradition!

Every culture has its own traditions. Whether it be Israel, Africa, China or the western Church, it does not take long to realize that tradition is an important foundation on which to operate one's life. Even those who say that they are "non-traditional" have, in reality, established their own new tradition. The issue, therefore, is not whether believers in Yeshua have traditions or not, but what the approach should be to these traditions.

1

This book is about certain traditions and customs that come directly from the Bible. One may note that these are usually identified as "Jewish" customs, but the fact is they are actually "biblical" customs. This means that these traditions are not only enriching to Jews, but that any Bible-believer can be blessed by an understanding of biblical culture. After all, every Christian knows that the Messiah lived as a Jew within the land of Israel. He had a Hebrew name, *Yeshua* ("Salvation"), and all of his earliest disciples were Jewish.

It is unfortunate that many Gentile believers in Yeshua have had little exposure to the Jewish roots of their own faith. The Jewish people also need to take a fresh look at the biblical/Jewish customs to understand their true meaning. Many in the modern Jewish community *are* being challenged to see the connection between Jewish culture and the New Testament. Today, hundreds of thousands of Jewish people believe that Yeshua is the Messiah and savior of mankind. The Jewish people are rediscovering that Yeshua is a Jew and that the New Testament is a Jewish book. As summed up by Dr. David Flusser of Jerusalem's Hebrew University:

> One should view Jesus against his Jewish background, the world of the Sages, to recognize and appreciate his great influence on those around him. Only thus shall we be able to understand how Christianity was formed. Jesus was part and parcel of the world of the Jewish Sages. He was no ignorant peasant, and his acquaintance with the Written and the Oral Law was considerable (*Jewish Sources in Early Christianity*, p. 18).

What better way to understand the Messiah than to study the context of the New Testament? The biblical customs are often the missing key to unlocking the depths of the Scriptures.

The Danger Of Customs

Why is it that many people are so ignorant of the customs of the Bible? Undoubtedly, many fear that an emphasis on *tradition* might lead some people away from the pure teaching of the Word of God. It is true that a spirit of *legalism* has all too often afflicted the church and synagogue. Isaiah the prophet rebuked his people for making the customs of Israel an empty expression (Isaiah 1). Rabbi *Moshe ben Maimon* (Maimonides), the great rabbi of the Middle Ages, similarly wrote:

> Man should try to understand why he is asked to observe precepts and customs; but even when he fails to fathom their reason he should not hastily pronounce them as trivial (Birnbaum, *Mishneh Torah*, Me'ilah 8:8).

Such ideals reflect the words of Yeshua. He denounced the emptiness and hypocrisy of those with a skewed view of the ancient traditions (Matthew 23:13–32).

This book is not about legalism. Salvation is not contingent upon keeping the Law or the customs, but is based on faith in Yeshua's atoning sacrifice and resurrection. Therefore, believers need to practice the freedom to choose and the withholding of judgment (Romans 14:13–15). Believers in Yeshua can have differing convictions in the area of lifestyle. However, this book will show that by practicing God's appointed customs, the believer in Yeshua will receive a multitude of spiritual blessings.

This book is about gaining an understanding of the biblical customs. Historically, the church has had a deficient understanding of its own roots because of its fear of legalism. What is even more ironic is that the Christian world has often rejected the biblical/Jewish customs and substituted non-biblical ones. The danger of legalism is always present, yet incredible blessing can be found through a biblically-based study of these God-appointed customs.

THE BALANCE OF CUSTOMS

This book seeks to present a balanced approach to understanding the importance and the danger of traditions. There are good traditions and there are bad traditions. Additionally, there is a good spirit and a wrong spirit in which one can approach the customs. These were certainly issues that faced the first Jewish and Gentile believers in Yeshua.

On the Jewish side, the acceptance of Yeshua did not mean that they *converted* to a new religion. The Jewish believers actually saw themselves as having received the fulfillment of what was spoken of in the Hebrew Scriptures. They understood this to mean that they were now Messianic Jews who would naturally continue in their God-given heritage. This fact is confirmed in a description of this Messianic Jewish community in the Book of Acts: "You see, brother [Saul], how many tens of thousands of believers there are among the Jews, and they are all zealots for the Torah" (Acts 21:20).

These first Jewish believers in Yeshua continued in the only lifestyle they knew: the Jewish life based on the Scriptures and customs consistent with the Bible. Their new understanding that Yeshua of Natzeret ("Nazareth") was the Messiah made them even more zealous for their traditions, as they understood the spiritual reasons behind them. Modern Messianic Jews frequently feel the same way and share the same enthusiasm.

The Gentile believer in Yeshua was not excluded. Saul wrote to many of them concerning their new life in Messiah: "Therefore, brothers, stand firm; and hold to the *traditions* [italics mine] you were taught by us, whether we spoke them or wrote them in a letter" (2 Thessalonians 2:15).

The first-century, non-Jewish believers in Yeshua understood many of the details of the Hebrew Scriptures and many of the traditions that enhanced them. An example of this is the cup shared at Messiah's last Passover *seder*. This element is not mandated in the Hebrew Scriptures, yet it became part of the tradition of Passover. The third cup is called the Cup of Redemption and, although it is a rabbinic tradition, it was blessed by Yeshua himself.

All traditions were weighed by the authority of the Bible, yet these believers were blessed as they understood the Jewish roots of their faith in Messiah. This is the balance that believers in Yeshua need to return to today. This book is an effort to bring out the spiritual richness of the biblical/Jewish traditions. It is a daunting task, but one that will enrich those believers who put forth the effort to study God's appointed customs.

Barney Kasdan
April 1996

Part 1

Biblical

Lifecycle

1

B'rit Milah

Covenant of Circumcision

THE HISTORICAL BACKGROUND

Then God said to Abraham, "As for you, you must keep my covenant, you and your descendants after you for the generations to come. This is my covenant with you and your descendants after you, the covenant you are to keep: Every male among you shall be circumcised. You are to undergo circumcision, and it will be the sign of the covenant between me and you. For the generations to come every male among you who is eight days old must be circumcised, including those born in your household or bought with money from a foreigner—those who are not your offspring. Whether born in your household or bought with your money, they must be circumcised. My covenant in your flesh is to be an everlasting covenant" (Genesis 17:9–13).

9

uneasy about this, the *mohel* (the one who circumcises) can be designated as the father's *shaliakh* ("representative"). The *mohel* is an observant Jew who is respected as a spiritual leader among his people. Many times the *mohel* will fast on the day of the *b'rit milah* to prepare his spirit for this *mitzvah* ("commandment"). The *mohel* must also have medical training in order to perform the procedure. For traditional Jews, training is available in special rabbinic programs at some hospitals.

Among the other participants at a traditional *b'rit milah* are those filling the symbolic roles for the ceremony. Each person supplies a beautiful link in the progression of this important event. For example, the first link in the chain is the *kvatterin* (the "godmother"). She is the one who takes the baby from the mother and brings him to the door of the room where the *b'rit milah* is to take place. Of all the official participants, the *kvatterin* is the only honor that goes to a woman. As the infant is brought to the doorway, the observers welcome the child with the familiar Hebrew phrase *Barukh habah b'shem Adonai* ("Blessed is he who comes in the Name of the Lord"). This verse, found in the Hallel (Psalm 118), is used in many Jewish liturgical prayers, especially for the holy days.

The next honored participant in the chain of the *b'rit milah* is the *kvatter* (the "godfather"). He is the one who takes the baby from the arms of the *kvatterin* and transfers him to the next delegated participant. This person stands next to the *kisey shel Eliyahu* ("chair of Elijah").

Elijah the Prophet plays an important role in many of the Jewish customs. This man of God lived during very difficult times in ancient Israel. Elijah believed that he was the only remaining Jew who was faithful to the covenant (see 1 Kings 19:10). Not only did Elijah have to contend with backslidden Israel, but also with the pagan wife (i.e., Jezebel) of a king. As a result of his faithfulness to the God of Israel, Elijah is given the honor of being remembered at several Jewish occasions. A special place-setting is set for Elijah at every Passover *seder* meal, because it is believed that he may come and drink from the extra cup, thereby announcing the coming of Messiah. It is also believed that Elijah attends the *b'rit milah* ceremony as the honored guest. No one actually sits in the chair of Elijah, but there is a person who stands by it and places the baby in the chair. It is believed that Elijah is present in spirit. Thus, the sign of the covenant (*b'rit milah*) takes place in the presence of the one who was the guardian of the covenant in his own generation.

The next participant fulfills the duty of *mikisey l'yad ha'av* ("from the chair to the hand of the father"). It is the task of this representative to pick up the baby from the chair of Elijah and to deliver him to the arms of his father. The father of the child, as if delegating his responsibility to an official representative, gives his son to the next person in the ceremony, the *sandek*. According to ancient Jewish tradition, the *sandek* is the one who actually holds the baby during the circumcision procedure. He is seated on a chair and holds the baby on a pillow, awaiting the work of the *mohel*. Before the start of the procedure, the *mohel* says the following blessing:

Barukh atah Adonai, eloheynu melekh ha'olam, asher kidshanu b'mitzvotav v'tzivanu al ha'milah.

Blessed art Thou, O Lord our God, King of the universe, who has sanctified us by his commandments and commanded us concerning circumcision.

At this time, the circumcision takes place. It normally takes only 10 to 15 minutes. While no anesthetic is used, the baby is often given a drop of sweet wine to help him through the ceremony. During the ritual, the father is obligated to recite the following:

Barukh atah Adonai, eloheynu melekh ha'olam, asher kidshanu b'mitzvotav v'tzivanu l'hakhniso bivrito shel Avraham avinu.

Blessed art Thou, O Lord our God, King of the universe who has sanctified us by his commandments and commanded us to bring our sons into the covenant of our father Abraham.

When the ritual is completed, the baby is wrapped up and given to another honored delegate, the *sandek sheni* ("second sandek"). This person is given the distinct privilege of holding the newly circumcised boy for the closing blessings of the ceremony. The blessings are chanted or read by the person who is the final link in the chain of tradition, the *mevoreykh* ("One who Blesses"). The first blessing is said over a cup of wine to represent the joy of the occasion:

Barukh atah Adonai, eloheynu melekh ha'olam, borey p'ri ha'gafen. Amen.

Blessed art Thou, O Lord our God, King of the universe, creator of the fruit of the vine. Amen.

After the family has sipped from the wine, the following blessing is read, which also serves the purpose of giving the child a Hebrew name:

Our God and God of our fathers, sustain this child in life and health and let him be known in the household of Israel by the name _____ *ben* _____ [Note: it is customary to explain the significance of the Hebrew name]. Cause the parents to rejoice in this child whom Thou hast entrusted to their care. As he has been brought into the covenant of Abraham, so may he be led to the study of Thy Torah, enter into a marriage worthy of Thy blessing, and live a life enriched with good deeds. Amen (Central Conference of American Rabbis, *Rabbi's Manual*, p. 11).

It is very important that the baby receive a Hebrew name that will be his identity for the synagogue and other Jewish ceremonies. In the Ashkenazi (European) tradition, the child is not to be named after a living relative, as this is considered bad luck. More appropriately, the baby receives the Hebrew name of a beloved deceased relative as an honor and to carry on the blessed memory of the loved-one. The Sephardic/Middle Eastern Jews do not hold to the same beliefs as the European-rooted community; therefore, the Sephardic community considers it an honor to name a boy after a living relative. The baby's Hebrew name is usually constructed by linking his first name with the first name of the father (e.g., David *ben* Boaz, David son of Boaz).

The final step in the ceremony of *b'rit milah* is the *seudah mitzvah* ("meal of the commandment"). This is the festive meal after the ceremony that celebrates the joy of a new life brought into the sign of the covenant. This may be an elaborate banquet or a relatively simple fellowship with friends and family. It is fitting to close by reminding everyone of the joy of their covenant relationship with the God of Abraham.

As vital as the *b'rit milah* ceremony was to the rabbis, they often reminded the community that the greater importance was to understand the spiritual lessons associated with this custom. In the Talmud (i.e., the Oral Law plus rabbinical discussions of the Oral Law), the rabbis asked what time a minor was entitled to his inheritance in the world to come. The answer was that a minor was entitled to his inheritance at his *b'rit milah* (*Babylonian Talmud*, Sanhedrin 110b). In the *Midrash* (a rabbinical commentary) on Exodus, the rabbis state that Abraham himself will sit at the gate of *Geyhinnom* ("Hell") and will not allow any circumcised Jew to enter (*Exodus Rabbah* 19.4).

The rabbis often pointed out that the Torah placed an important spiritual emphasis on the significance of *b'rit milah*. Circumcision is a reminder that one's spirit is to be submitted to God.

> And now, O Israel, what does the LORD your God ask of you but to fear the LORD your God, to walk in all his ways, to love him, to serve the LORD your God with all your heart and with all your soul, and to observe the LORD's commands and decrees that I am giving you today for your own good? To the LORD your God belong the heavens, even the highest heavens, the earth and everything in it. Yet the LORD set his affection on your forefathers and loved them, and he chose you, their descendants, above all the nations, as it is today. Circumcise your hearts, therefore, and do not be

stiff-necked any longer (Deuteronomy 10:12–16; cf., Jeremiah 4:4; 9:25–26).

In a parallel passage, it was shown that the circumcised heart is a spiritual work that can only be performed by God. Whereas physical circumcision is the removal of the flesh, spiritual circumcision involves the removal of that which is unclean in one's spirit.

> The LORD your God will circumcise your hearts and the hearts of your descendants, so that you may love him with all your heart and with all your soul, and live (Deuteronomy 30:6).

Within traditional Judaism, the question arose regarding what to do with Gentiles who desired to join themselves to Israel's faith. This was not uncommon in the biblical and talmudic periods, as seen in such cases as Rahab and Ruth. While the Bible does not define the exact requirements for a Gentile to convert to Judaism, the rabbis described them in detail. In addition to adopting a belief in the one true God of Israel, a Gentile was required to live a Torah-lifestyle. According to the great rabbi, Hillel (first century C.E.), initiation into the household of Israel had to include three things: sacrifice in the Temple, *mikveh* (ritual immersion) and circumcision (for men). It is important to realize that these three conditions were not universally accepted. Rabbi Joshua, of the same time period, differed with Hillel. He said *mikveh* was required but circumcision was not required (*Babylonian Talmud*, Yevamot 46a). This issue directly impacted the Messianic Jewish movement. Many of the same opinions were discussed at the Jerusalem Council, described in Acts 15.

RELEVANCE TO THE NEW TESTAMENT

Many of the customs pertaining to *b'rit milah* will sound familiar to those acquainted with the New Testament. Of course, initially the New Testament was written by Jews to a largely Jewish audience, about Jewish concepts. Accordingly, the New Testament presents a view of *b'rit milah* as a custom that can be appreciated and followed when one has the proper biblical balance. Similar to the Torah injunctions, the New Testament reaffirms the importance of the spiritual lessons of circumcision.

> For in him [Messiah], bodily, lives the fullness of all that God is. And it is in union with him that you have been made full—he is the head of every rule and authority. Also it was in union with him that you were circumcised with a circumcision not done by human hands, but accomplished by stripping away the old nature's control over the body . . . (Colossians 2:9–11).

The circumcision of the flesh is of value as a custom appointed by God; however, the greatest value is in the lesson of spiritual circumcision. Unlike the earthly *b'rit milah*, the circumcised heart must be a work of God through the Messiah. Hence, when understood within its spiritual context, it becomes clear that the New Testament never denounced the custom of *b'rit milah* (see Romans 2:17, 28–29).

The New Testament recounts more than one *b'rit milah* ceremony. The Gospel of Luke relates the amazing details surrounding the birth of the man known as *Yokhanan* ("John" the Baptizer). His parents, *Z'kharyah* ("Zechariah")and *Elisheva* ("Elizabeth"), were elderly. Therefore, Z'kharyah doubted that he could father a child, and the angel Gabriel struck him with silence until the birth of his son. Finally, at the birth of *Yokhanan* a strange turn of events took place.

> The time arrived for Elisheva [Elizabeth] to have her baby, and she gave birth to a son. Her neighbors and relatives heard how good Adonai had been to her, and they rejoiced with her. On the eighth day, they came to do the child's b'rit-milah. They were about to name him Z'kharyah, after his father, when his mother spoke up and said, "No, he is to be called Yochanan." They said to her, "None of your relatives has that name,"

and they made signs to his father to find out what he wanted him called. He motioned for a writing tablet, and to everyone's surprise he wrote, "His name is Yochanan." At the moment, his power of speech returned, and his first words were a b'rakhah [blessing] to God. All their neighbors were awestruck; and throughout the hill country of Y'hudah [Judah], people talked about all these things. Everyone who heard of them said to himself, "What is this child going to be?" For clearly the hand of Adonai was with him (Luke 1:57–66).

This was a traditional *b'rit milah* ceremony, as was practiced in Jerusalem during the first century. Presumably, all the customary elements of the ritual were present: the friends, the honored participants, the *mohel* and the *mevoreykh*. During the naming of the son, there was a controversy about which name to use. In this Sephardic, middle eastern setting, it would be more traditional to name a son in honor of a living relative. *Z'kharyah ben Z'kharyah* would have been one obvious choice for a traditional name in this first- century culture. Yet, because of the angel's message to the parents, they knew they must name him *Yokhanan ben Z'kharyah* ("John son of Zechariah"). Indeed, the guests were quite surprised as there was no family member by that name. However, it is always a wise policy to follow God's clear instructions. Perhaps *Yokhanan* ("God is gracious") was a better prophetic name for this messenger to Israel, since it was he who presented the message to prepare for the coming Messiah. Nonetheless, the *b'rit milah* ceremony ended and *Yokhanan* developed into a man who was used for God's purpose.

Several other passages in the New Testament speak of the custom of *b'rit milah*, both from historical and theological viewpoints. Even Yeshua of *Natzeret* had a traditional *b'rit milah*. Luke's Gospel states:

One the eighth day, when it was time for his b'rit-milah, he was given the name Yeshua, which is what the angel had called him before his conception (Luke 2:21).

The custom of *b'rit milah* continued with the early Messianic Jews, as they rightfully considered themselves part of the covenant with their father Abraham. It never entered their minds that they had somehow "converted" to a new religion. Actually, they were even more zealous for their Jewish heritage and customs (see Acts 21:20). Therefore, Saul of Tarsus (Paul was his Greek name) confirmed, as a part of his testimony, that his parents brought him into the sign of the covenant with the eighth-day *b'rit milah* (see Philippians 3:5).

Acts 16:1–3 describes Timothy's circumcision. Timothy, who was born Jewish, was not raised in a traditional way. Since Saul desired to take Timothy with him into the Jewish communities, he made sure that Timothy had a *b'rit milah*, even though it was at a later stage of Timothy's life.

This last point often creates some theological confusion among many non-Jewish believers in Yeshua. It is often taught and preached that Saul held an anti-circumcision viewpoint. After all, he warned the Galatian believers not to take the sign of circumcision or else they would be under danger of judgment from God. Saul wrote:

> What the Messiah has freed us for is freedom! Therefore, stand firm, and don't let yourselves be tied up again to a yoke of slavery. Mark my words—I, Sha'ul, tell you that if you undergo b'rit-milah the Messiah will be of no advantage to you at all! Again, I warn you: any man who undergoes *b'rit milah* is obligated to observe the entire Torah (Galatians 5:1–3)!

The context of this letter to the Galatians is often overlooked. It is vital to remember that Saul was addressing non-Jews who were seeking to earn merit before God by following the customs. The next verse clarified the problem:

> You who are trying to be declared righteous by God through legalism have severed yourselves from the Messiah! You have fallen away from God's grace (Galatians 5:4)!

Saul never intended to imply that it was somehow inherently wrong for believers in Yeshua to follow *b'rit milah* as a custom. If this were the case, how could one possibly explain Saul's circumcision of Timothy? The two-fold issue is this: first, circumcision is a sign of the Abrahamic Covenant for Jewish descendants of the patriarch. Hence, it is a non-issue for the Gentile community since they technically are not related to the physical aspects of the Abrahamic Covenant. While Saul circumcised Timothy, a Jew, he refused to be pressured into circumcising Titus, who was not Jewish (see Galatians 2:3).

Secondly, one must examine the context of the verses warning the Galatians to reject the requirement of *b'rit milah*. The context made it clear that they were under the false belief that they could somehow be justified (saved) by submitting to a *b'rit milah*. Saul refutes this false doctrine, since neither Jew nor Gentile will ever be justified by the works of the Torah (see Romans 3:20). Hence, there is a balance in the New Testament that affirms the proper perspective of *b'rit milah*. Although ritual circumcision does nothing to justify one before a holy God, it is still a sign of the Abrahamic Covenant for Messianic Jews. With a clear understanding that justification is accomplished only by faith in the risen Messiah, believers in Yeshua are free to follow the custom of *b'rit milah*.

This issue of the relationship of *b'rit milah* to the Messianic believer (Jew or Gentile) was so controversial in the first century that a special council convened in Jerusalem to discuss it. After hearing the various sides, the leaders of the early Messianic movement came to a consensus and made the following declaration:

> The emissaries and the elders met to look into this matter. After lengthy debate, Kefa [Peter] got up and said to them, "Brothers, you yourselves know that a good while back, God chose me from among you to be the one by whose mouth the Goyim should hear the message of the Good News and come to trust. And God, who knows the heart, bore them witness by giving the Ruach HaKodesh to them, just as he did to

us; that is, he made no distinction between us and them, but cleansed their heart by trust. So why are you putting God to the test now by placing a yoke on the neck of the talmidim which neither our fathers nor we have had the strength to bear? No, it is through the love and kindness of the Lord Yeshua that we trust and are delivered—and it's the same with them" (Acts 15:6–11).

As with the passage from Galatians, the controversy is really two-fold. First, what is the basis of justification before God, for both Jew and Gentile? It is agreed that faith in the Messiah's death and resurrection are the essentials, not adherence to any particular custom. The second problem addressed is one that modern believers do not often consider. With the Messianic Jewish movement spreading among the Gentiles, the Gentiles had to adapt from a pagan lifestyle to a Messianic one. This sounds strange to many people today. Usually believers are faced with the exact opposite question. How can a Jew accept Yeshua the Messiah and fit into the Gentile church structure? In the first century, the proverbial sandal was on the other foot. How did the Jerusalem Council address the issue of the place of the non-Jewish believer in the Messianic movement?

Then the whole assembly kept still as they listened to Bar-Nabba [Barnabas] and Sha'ul tell what signs and miracles God had done through them among the Gentiles. Ya'akov [James] broke the silence to reply, "Brothers," he said, "hear what I have to say. Shim'on [Simon] has told in detail what God did when he first began to show his concern for taking from among the Goyim a people to bear his name. And the words of the Prophets are in complete harmony with this—for it is written,

"After this, I will return; and I will rebuild the fallen tent of David. I will rebuild its ruins, I will restore it, so that the rest of mankind may seek

one's best consultant regarding these details. Whether simple or elaborate, the most important element is the spiritual focus of the ceremony. The following is an example of a *b'rit milah* service:

With all the family and guests gathered in the room, the mother is seated in a chair outside the door holding the child. She passes the child to the godmother (*kvatterin*) who brings the baby to the entrance of the room as the leader declares:

Barukh habah b'shem Adonai

Blessed is he who comes in the name of the Lord.

The leader continues, saying:

The rite of circumcision has been enjoined upon us as a sign of our covenant with God, as it is written:

The leader reads Genesis 17:9–14, then continues:

As Messianic Jews, we follow the example of Messiah Yeshua and the first Jewish believers.

The leader reads Luke 2:21. This would be an appropriate place to give a short message regarding the significance of *b'rit milah* for Messianic Jews, perhaps using other relevant Scriptures.

The godfather (*kvatter*) takes the child from the *kvatterin* and gives the boy to the person watching over the seat of Elijah. This person briefly sets the baby on the chair. He is then picked up by a second person who hands the child to the father.

The father says:

In conformity with sacred Jewish observance, I present my son for the covenant of circumcision.

Barukh atah Adonai, eloheynu melekh ha'olam, asher kidshanu b'mitzvotav v'tzivanu l'hakhniso bivrito shel Avraham avinu.

Blessed art Thou, O Lord our God, King of the universe who has sanctified us by his commandments and commanded us to bring our sons into the covenant of Abraham our father.

The father gives his son to the *sandek* (if one is used) who is seated in a chair with a pillow on his lap. This person holds the child while the circumcision is performed by the *mohel*.

Just before the circumcision is performed, the leader reads the following:

Barukh atah Adonai, eloheynu melekh ha'olam, asher kidshanu b'mitzvotav v'tzivanu al ha'milah.

Blessed art Thou, O Lord our God, King of the universe who has sanctified us by his commandments and commanded us concerning the rite of circumcision.

After the circumcision, the leader picks up the wine cup and chants:

Barukh atah Adonai, eloheynu melekh ha'olam, borey p'ri ha'gafen. Amen.

Blessed art Thou, O Lord our God, King of the universe who creates the fruit of the vine. Amen.

As the parents sip the wine, the leader continues:

Our God and God of our fathers, sustain this child in life and health and let him be known in the household of Israel by the name _____ *ben* _____ [Note: it is customary to explain the significance of the Hebrew name]. Cause the parents to rejoice in this child whom Thou hast entrusted to their care. As he has been brought into the covenant of Abraham, so may he be led to the study of Thy Torah, enter into a marriage worthy of Thy blessing, and live a life enriched with good deeds. Amen (Central Conference of American Rabbis, *Rabbi's Manual*, p. 11).

Although *b'rit milah* does not relate to girls, the above prayer serves as a good model for a naming or dedication ceremony. However, instead of using the word *ben* ("son"), the word *bat* ("daughter") should be used. This is often done at the first congregational service that the baby girl is able to attend.

After this naming prayer, a personal prayer should be said for the child and their family. This prayer should affirm that the child will be brought up to know Messiah Yeshua at a very early age. An important memento of the joyous occasion can be the beautiful Messianic certificate for either B'*rit Milah* or Child Dedication (see below; also see Conclusion for how to obtain one). Finally, the family will probably want to follow the ceremony with a joyous meal, at home or elsewhere, to celebrate the new life. *Mazel Tov!* (Congratulations!)

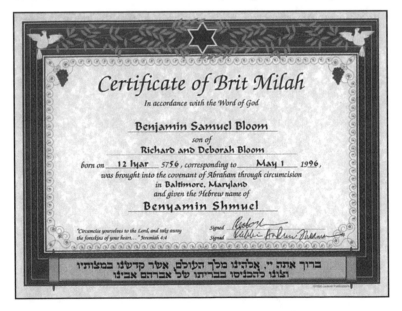

Certificate of Brit Milah

In accordance with the Word of God

Benjamin Samuel Bloom

son of

Richard and Deborah Bloom

born on __12 Iyar__ 5756, *corresponding to* __May 1__ 1996, *was brought into the covenant of Abraham through circumcision in* **Baltimore, Maryland** *and given the Hebrew name of*

Benyamin Shmuel

2

Pidyon Ha'ben

Redemption of the Firstborn

THE HISTORICAL BACKGROUND

After the Lord brings you into the land of the Canaanites and gives it to you, as he promised on oath to you and your forefathers, you are to give over to the Lord the first offspring of every womb. All the firstborn males of your livestock belong to the Lord. Redeem with a lamb every firstborn donkey, but if you do not redeem it, break its neck. Redeem every firstborn among your sons. In days to come, when your son asks you, "What does this mean?" say to him, "With a mighty hand the Lord brought us out of Egypt, out of the land of slavery. When Pharaoh stubbornly refused to let us go, the Lord killed every firstborn in Egypt, both man and animal. This is why I sacrifice to the Lord the first male offspring of every womb and redeem each of my firstborn sons" (Exodus 13:11–15).

What an amazing event it was! What other nation in all of history can claim that their God brought them from slavery to freedom? It is of course a long story, spanning over 400 years, describing how Abraham's descendants ended up in this foreign land. Those familiar with the Bible are acquainted with the famine in Canaan, the selling of Joseph by his brothers and the other *coincidences* that eventually brought all of the children of Israel to Egypt. The early chapters of the book of Exodus recount the miraculous deliverance of the Jewish people from the oppression of Pharaoh. This deliverance has been celebrated annually in the Passover *seder* meal for the last 3500 years.

A lesser known biblical custom associated with the deliverance from Egypt is *pidyon ha'ben* ("redemption of the firstborn"). This custom might appear somewhat strange, but as it is scrutinized more closely, one begins to appreciate its beautiful symbolism. A number of interesting parallels can be made between *pidyon ha'ben* and the spiritual lessons of redemption.

As the people stood at the threshold of their new land, they could appreciate a custom that illustrated the process by which they got there. They were a redeemed people, both physically and spiritually, as they walked with the God of their fathers. The tenth plague brought death to all firstborn in Egypt, but the Israelites were spared because they followed God's dictates. The Israelites placed the blood of the sacrificial lamb on the doorposts of their houses (see Exodus 12). By so doing, God promised that he would *pass over* their dwelling places (Exodus 12:12). As a result, God said that all the firstborn animals and sons belonged to him. It was very clear to that generation of Israelites that they owed their firstborn sons to the Lord. Those sons, having been saved by God's hand, were now obligated to be his full-time servants and priests.

This consecration of the firstborn evolved into an even more interesting symbolic custom. For several years after the departure from Egypt, these firstborn sons served as the priesthood of the Jewish nation. However, as God revealed more of his plan for his people, he designated an entire tribe of Israel for this holy purpose—the sons of Levi (see Numbers 8:14–18). This presented an interesting problem regarding what to do with the previously appointed firstborn sons. The answer is found in the Torah. God specified that the firstborn sons be redeemed (bought back) for service other than full-time priesthood. God spoke to Aaron, the high priest, saying:

> Everything in Israel that is devoted to the LORD is yours. The first offspring of every womb, both man and animal, that is offered to the LORD is yours. But you must redeem every firstborn son and every firstborn male of unclean animals. When they are a month old, you must redeem them at the redemption price set at five shekels of silver, according to the sanctuary shekel, which weighs twenty gerahs (Numbers 18:14–16).

This law did not apply to any firstborn son who also happened to be from the tribe of Levi. The firstborn sons of the tribe of Levi were obligated to be God's full-time priests and could not be redeemed for any other purpose. Through the symbolism of this God-appointed custom, the children of Israel always remembered where they came from and to whom they belonged. *Pidyon ha'ben* is a picture of God's redemptive love that believers in Yeshua should never forget.

TRADITIONAL JEWISH OBSERVANCE

Since the days of Moses, the custom of *pidyon ha'ben* has been an important event in the biblical/Jewish lifecycle.

As mentioned in the Torah (Numbers 18:16), the timing of *pidyon ha'ben* is one-month after a boy's birth. Since traditional Jews would not want to waste any time, the ceremony usually takes place on the 31st day after birth. In biblical times this would require the father to take his infant son into the Tabernacle or Temple. The father was obligated to find a godly priest, from the sons of Aaron (a Cohen) or from the tribe of

Levi (the larger priestly tribe). As the father presented his son to the priest, the Cohen or Levite would ask him specifically, "What is your preference—to give me your firstborn son or to  redeem him for five shekels, as you are commanded to do in the Torah?" (Olitzky and Isaacs, *The Second How to Handbook for Jewish Living*, p. 62). The father would then state his intention, either to give up his son for priestly service or to redeem him.

At this point, it was important for there to be an official exchange of money. The exact amount is stated in the Torah, namely five shekels of silver. The child was obviously worth a bit more than this, but it is the spiritual symbolism that was always the more important issue. As the redemption money exchanged hands, certain Hebrew blessings were chanted by the priest over the boy.

Barukh atah Adonai, eloheynu melekh ha'olam, asher kidshanu b'mitzvotav v'tzivanu al pidyon ha'ben. Amen.

Blessed art Thou, O Lord our God, King of the universe who has sanctified us by his commandments and commanded us concerning the redemption of the firstborn. Amen.

Barukh atah Adonai, eloheynu melekh ha'olam, shehekheyanu v'kiymanu v'higiyanu lazman ha'zeh. Amen.

Blessed art Thou, O Lord our God, King of the universe who has kept us in life, sustained us and brought us to this occasion. Amen.

A *kiddush* cup (wine goblet) would then be blessed and, as is often the case at Jewish events, a great celebratory meal would follow. The entire *pidyon ha'ben* ceremony is relatively simple in its format yet quite powerful in its spiritual message.

Traditional Jews still follow this custom despite the fact that Israel no longer has a Temple or a priesthood. However, through the family names, Jews have kept track of which families are descended from the tribe of Levi (Levy, Levitz, etc.) and from the house of Aaron (Cohen, Katz, even Kasdan). Today, for example, a traditional family would seek out a Cohen in the synagogue and exchange five silver dollars or specially minted "Pidyon Ha'ben Coins" from Israel. The *pidyon ha'ben* ceremony has often been neglected by less traditional Jews who view such customs as irrelevant to modern Jewish life. However, it still has some wonderful truth for believers in Yeshua.

RELEVANCE TO THE NEW TESTAMENT

Since the New Testament takes place within the first-century Jewish community, it records the *pidyon ha'ben* ceremony of the Messiah.

> When the time came for their purification according to the Torah of Moshe, they took him up to Yerushalayim [Jerusalem] to present him to Adonai (as it is written in the Torah of Adonai, "Every firstborn male is to be consecrated to Adonai") and also to offer a sacrifice of a pair of doves or two young pigeons, as required by the Torah of Adonai (Luke 2:22–24).

As stipulated in the Torah, Yosef ("Joseph") and Miryam ("Mary") brought their newborn baby boy to the Temple to fulfill their obligations. This obligation was two-fold: first, to ceremonially cleanse the mother with the proper sacrifices (Leviticus 12:1–8). The family of Yeshua was not wealthy, and therefore presented the less expensive offering of the pigeons. The second part of the obligation was redeeming the firstborn son through the *pidyon ha'ben* ritual. The child

Yeshua was not exempt from this redemption. Although he was the Messiah, he was not from the levitical tribe. In actuality, the Scriptures predicted that the Messiah would be from another leading tribe—Judah (see Genesis 49:10). Yeshua's *pidyon ha'ben* ceremony is described in Luke's Gospel:

> There was in Yerushalayim a man named Shim'on [Simeon]. This man was a tzaddik [righteous one], he was devout, he waited eagerly for God to comfort Israel, and the Ruach HaKodesh was upon him. It had been revealed to him by the Ruach HaKodesh that he would not die before he had seen the Messiah of Adonai. Prompted by the Spirit, he went into the Temple courts; and when the parents brought in the child Yeshua to do for him what the Torah required, Shim'on took him in his arms, made a *b'rakhah* [blessing] to God, and said,

> "Now, Adonai, according to your word, your servant is at peace as you let him go; for I have seen with my own eyes your yeshu'ah [salvation], which you prepared in the presence of all peoples—a light that will bring revelation to the Goyim and glory to your people Israel."

> Yeshua's father and mother were marvelling [sic] at the things Shim'on was saying about him (Luke 2:25–33).

As Yeshua's family worshipped in the Temple, they undoubtedly realized that they needed a godly Cohen to officiate the ritual for their son. They found such a man in *Shim'on* ("Simeon"), who was not only devout but was also a man looking expectantly for the consolation of Israel (i.e., the coming of Messiah). Was it only a coincidence that *Yosef* and *Miryam* found this godly priest, or could it be that they sought him out knowing that he was a Cohen with a "Messianic" vision?

In accordance with ancient tradition, the young couple placed their son in the arms of the priest who asked the relevant questions about their desire to redeem their boy. As the shekels were exchanged, the Cohen would "bless God" with the traditional blessings. *Yosef* and *Miryam* were amazed as they heard the priest add a few of his own prophetic comments inspired by the *Ruakh HaKodesh*. This son would be *yeshu'ah* (a word play on the *name* "Yeshua"), salvation for many in Israel as well as a light to non-Jews.

It seems that *Yosef* and *Miryam* certainly got their five shekels worth from this priest, as he turned to the parents:

Shim'on blessed them and said to the child's mother, Miryam,

"This child will cause many in Israel to fall and to rise, he will become a sign whom people will speak against; moreover, a sword will pierce your own heart too.

All this will happen in order to reveal many people's inmost thoughts" (Luke 2:34–35).

How thrilling it must have been to witness this *pidyon ha'ben* ceremony. This particular son was to be presented to all of Israel as the Messiah. Many would naturally rejoice at this fact and bless God for his faithfulness to his covenants (see Luke 2:36–38). However, this son would certainly be controversial among many in Israel. *Miryam's* heart would be emotionally pierced as she saw the division among her own people as they debated the Messianic claims of her son, Yeshua of *Natzeret*.

This prophecy of *Shim'on* has certainly proven true. Even today, Yeshua is a source of controversy and division in the household of Israel. While it is true that many in the nation have rejected his clear proclamations of being the Messiah, it has always been a split decision. Many other Jews (including approximately 200,000 today) have embraced Yeshua. There is a thriving remnant of Messianic Jews today who stand as a testimony that Yeshua has brought spiritual salvation to all who call on his name.

It is fitting that the earliest presentation of Yeshua to the Jewish people was in Jerusalem at his *pidyon ha'ben* ceremony.

The one who would bring spiritual redemption through his death and resurrection submitted to this God-appointed custom. This redemption of Messiah was the greatest lesson to be learned from *pidyon ha'ben*, as the Jewish disciple *Shim'on Kefa* (Simon Peter) wrote:

> You should be aware that the ransom paid to free you from the worthless way of life which your fathers passed on to you did not consist of anything perishable like silver or gold; on the contrary, it was the costly bloody sacrificial death of the Messiah, as of a lamb without defect or spot (1 Peter 1:18–19).

This is the ultimate fulfillment of what *pidyon ha'ben* symbolizes. As the Jewish people were physically redeemed from the slavery of Egypt, so those who believe in God's Messiah have been redeemed from spiritual bondage. Believers in Yeshua have been bought, not just with the five silver shekels, but with the very blood of the Messiah. Now believers are redeemed to walk in newness of life.

Every one needs to ask themselves if they have received that gift of redemption and if they are walking in the new life that Messiah purchased for them. May all believers appreciate the spiritual lessons illustrated in *pidyon ha'ben* as they walk with the one who has redeemed them, *Yeshua HaMashiakh*.

PRACTICAL GUIDE FOR A MESSIANIC PIDYON HA'BEN CEREMONY

The following is a suggested ceremony that may be adapted to fit the desires and convictions of the parents. The spiritual lessons and one's freedom in the *Ruakh HaKodesh* are the most important rules for guidance.

INTRODUCTION

It would be good to have the Cohen give some background of this ceremony and what it means to believers in Yeshua the Messiah.

The father gives his son to a designated Cohen and says the following:

This is the firstborn son of his mother, and God has directed us to redeem him, as it is written in the Torah.

The father reads Exodus 13:11–15 and then places five silver coins in his hand.
The Cohen says:

Which do you prefer, to give me your son or redeem him?

The father says:

I wish to redeem him with the equivalent of five shekels and thus fulfill my obligation in the Torah.

The father reads Numbers 18:15–16.

The Cohen accepts the payment for redemption and returns the son to the arms of the father as the father says:

Barukh atah Adonai, eloheynu melekh ha'olam, asher kidshanu b'mitzvotav v'tzivanu al pidyon ha'ben. Amen.

Blessed art Thou, O Lord our God, King of the universe who has sanctified us by his commandments and commanded us concerning the redemption of the firstborn. Amen.

The father and mother thank God for the gift of the new life entrusted to them:

Barukh atah Adonai, eloheynu melekh ha'olam, shehekheyanu v'kiymanu v'higiyanu lazman ha'zeh. Amen.

Blessed art Thou, O Lord our God, King of the universe who has kept us in life, sustained us and brought us to this time. Amen. (Some Messianic believers add "*b'shem Yeshua HaMashiakh*, in the name of Yeshua the Messiah").

As the Cohen holds the coins, he makes the following declaration:

I accept the five shekels and hereby declare your son redeemed. May he be granted a full and blessed life, living in devotion to our God. May this redemption ceremony remind us all of our need for the spiritual redemption found in the Messiah, Yeshua, as it is written in the New Covenant.

The Cohen reads 1 Peter 1:17–21 and then blesses the child with the following:

Y'simkha elohim k'efrayim v'khim-nasheh.

May God make you like Ephraim and Manasseh (Genesis 48:20).

Y'varekh'kha Adonai v'yishm'rekha, yaer Adonai panav eylekha vikhu-nekha, yisa Adonai panav eylekha v'yaseym l'kha shalom.

The LORD bless you and keep you. The LORD make His face to shine upon you and be gracious to you. The LORD turn his face toward you, and give you peace. Amen (Numbers 6:24–26).

Mazel tov! Congratulations for this son which God has blessed you with!

To celebrate the occasion, a joyous meal can be held after the ceremony.

3

Bar/Bat Mitzvah

Son/Daughter of the Commandment

The Historical Background

> My son, if you accept my words and store up my
>   commands within you,
> turning your ear to wisdom and applying your heart to
>   understanding,
> and if you call out for insight and cry aloud for under-
>   standing,
> and if you look for it as for silver and search for it as for
>   hidden treasure,
> then you will understand the fear of the LORD and find
>   the knowledge of God (Proverbs 2:1–5).

One of the best known customs of the Jewish people is that of
Bar/Bat Mitzvah. Whether or not one is from a Jewish background,
most people realize that the Bar/Bat Mitzvah is an important step in
the life of a Jewish child. As the Hebrew/Aramaic name implies (bar
is Aramaic for "son"; bat is Hebrew for "daughter"; mitzvah is Hebrew
for "commandment"), this is a milestone in the life of a Jewish child.
It is a time when the child takes responsibility for his or her own
religious life. It is considered the biblical age of accountability.
The child crosses that precarious gap between childhood and
adolescence, with its requisite duties.

The historical background of the Bar/Bat Mitzvah custom is
somewhat more difficult to track than many other traditions.
This is primarily because there is no specific reference to the
ceremony in the Hebrew Scriptures. However, there are dozens of verses that support the idea that there is an age of
accountability to the commandments of the Lord. Some
would find it ironic that the most detailed account of a Bar
Mitzvah in the Bible is actually in the New Testament, at the
"Bar Mitzvah" ceremony for Messiah Yeshua.

However, much can be learned from the historical writings
of the rabbis, through their various commentaries on the Scriptures. The ancient rabbis considered either age 12 or 13 to be
both the age of accountability and the age of physical maturity.
At this time, the child is responsible to start taking upon himself
certain of the commandments and duties, such as celebrating
the feasts of the Torah (see Babylonian Talmud, Kiddushin 16b).
Up until that time, the parents take full responsibility for the
child's actions, including vows, discipline problems and religious training (Jerusalem Talmud, Nedarim 5:6). At age 12 (or some
say 13), this relationship begins to change. Another talmudic
quote states that this transitional time of life makes the child a
Bar Mitzvah (Babylonian Talmud, Pirke Avot 5:24).

Although the exact time of this change in duties was
debated, the Talmud makes the recommendation that the
child start observing the feasts one year prior to becoming an
official Bar Mitzvah (Babylonian Talmud, Yoma 82a). The ancient
commentaries note that, in the days of the Jerusalem Temple,
the boy or girl would appear before the rabbis for a special
blessing (Jerusalem Talmud, Sofrim 18:7).

It seems that the official ceremony, now called a Bar Mitzvah, did not become commonplace until the Middle Ages. At the age of 13, a Jewish boy would have completed his early Hebrew and religious studies, and would therefore begin to participate in the Sabbath synagogue service to fulfill this requirement. A more modern adaptation gives Jewish girls the same honor, usually at the age 12, since it is presumed that they mature more quickly than their male counterparts.

The main purpose of the Bar/Bat Mitzvah ceremony is to be an official initiation into adolescence and Jewish religious duties.

TRADITIONAL JEWISH OBSERVANCE

Preparing for such a transition in life does not happen overnight. Indeed, most Jewish children spend several years in synagogue and Hebrew school studies, gradually working toward the goal of becoming a Bar/Bat Mitzvah. This course of study includes the Hebrew language, but is often supplemented with studies in Jewish history, tradition and Bible. The years of preparation are culminated with the Bar/Bat Mitzvah ceremony at a special synagogue service on a Sabbath close to the child's 13th birthday (12th for the girl).

The actual ceremony is quite beautiful and significant. Symbolic of his or her new responsibilities, the boy or girl is prepared to actually lead a significant part of the synagogue service. Specifically, the child has mastered various parts of the liturgical service that, depending on the capabilities of the young student, may include such Hebrew prayers as the Sh'ma (Deuteronomy 6:4), the Amidah (18 Benedictions) and various Psalms. In addition to leading part of the service, the Bar/Bat Mitzvah also chants the traditional weekly reading from the Torah and the Prophets.

Immediately before the Scripture readings, the child is given a very special honor. The cantor, or the father of the child, opens the ark containing the Torah scroll and places it in the arms of the Bar/Bat Mitzvah. After the appropriate blessings are chanted, a holy processional starts as the child walks the scroll down the aisles of the synagogue. It is common for people to show their reverence for the Word of God by reaching out and touching the mantle covering the Torah with their *tallitot* (prayer shawls) or *siddurim* (prayer books). The congregates face the direction of the scroll out of respect for God's Word, as the B*ar/Bat Mitzvah* marches up to the *bimah* (pulpit or platform). The Torah is opened and the B*ar/Bat Mitzvah* chants the opening blessings:

> *Barukh atah Adonai, eloheynu melekh ha'olam, asher bakhar banu mikal ha'amim, v'natan lanu et torato. Barukh atah Adonai, noteyn ha'torah. Amen.*

> Blessed art Thou, O Lord our God, King of the universe, who has chosen us from all peoples and given us the Torah. Blessed art Thou, O Lord, giver of the Torah. Amen.

The weekly Torah portion is traditionally blessed by seven readers, each one blessing a section of the reading. This would be followed by the Bar/Bat Mitzvah, who does the blessings and then reads from the Torah. The child does not just read the passage in Hebrew (which is challenge enough), but also chants the musical notes that accompany the reading, called the cantillation. These melodies are believed to date back to the time of Moses (see Deuteronomy 31:19–22), and were codified in the Masoretic text of the Hebrew Scriptures.

When the reading from the Torah scroll is finished, the B*ar/Bat Mitzvah* chants the following blessing:

> *Barukh atah Adonai, eloheynu melekh ha'olam, asher natan lanu torat emet, v'chayey olam nata b'tokheynu. Barukh atah Adonai, noteyn ha'torah. Amen.*

> Blessed art Thou, O Lord our God, King of the universe, who has given us the Torah of truth, and planted everlasting life in our midst. Blessed art Thou, O Lord, giver of the Torah. Amen.

The reading of the Haftarah (from the verb l'haftir, "to dismiss") is called the maftir (from the same verb), because it occurs near the end of the synagogue service. The Haftarah is a selection from the prophetic writings that elucidates a theme found in the Torah portion. The reading begins with the last three verses from the Torah portion in order to avoid the impression that the Haftarah is equal in importance to the Torah and deserving of its own separate reader. The Bar/Bat Mitzvah child reads these maftir verses in the Torah, gives the closing blessing, and segues into the Haftarah. The child has a special challenge, as he or she must read the extra Hebrew plus chant a cantillation exclusively for the prophetic reading. Before the reader begins this last section, the following blessing is chanted:

Barukh atah Adonai, eloheynu melekh ha'olam, asher bakhar binvi'im tovim, v'ratzah b'divreyhem ha'ne'emarim be'emet. Barukh atah Adonai, ha'bokheyr ba'torah uvmoshe avdo, uvyisraeyl amo, uvinvi'ey ha'emet va'tzedek. Amen.

Blessed art Thou, O Lord our God, King of the universe, who has selected good prophets, taking delight in their words which were spoken in truth. Blessed art Thou, O Lord, who has chosen the Torah, Thy servant Moses, Thy people Israel, and the prophets of truth and righteousness. Amen.

All eyes are on the Bar/Bat Mitzvah child as he or she chants the traditional reading from the Prophets. After this reading (which may be as short as a few verses or as long as two chapters) is finished, the child chants the closing blessing for the Haftarah portion.

This is too lengthy to quote here (refer to Scherman, *The Rabbinical Council of America Edition of The Artscroll Siddur*—see bibliography—or any other traditional *siddur*), but includes such thoughts as blessing God for his faithfulness, mercy to Zion and even a prayer that Elijah would come soon to announce the days of Messiah.

Having accomplished his or her primary task of chanting the Scriptures, the child presents the last part of the ceremony—the *drashah* ("sermon" or "teaching"). This is more commonly known as the B*ar/Bat Mitzvah* speech where the child gives a mini-sermon and thanks family and friends for participating in this joyous occasion. The child expounds upon the readings and how the passage is meaningful to his or her life. It can be quite inspiring to hear such comments from a teenager.

The ceremony usually closes with the customary greetings and best wishes from family and friends. The synagogue may make various presentations to the child (e.g., certificates, a prayer shawl (for a boy), or a Bible). Girls often receive their first pair of sabbath candlesticks. Quite often, the synagogue service is followed by a reception or party in honor of the new B*ar/Bat Mitzvah*. Gifts, food and Israeli folk-dancing usually abound to celebrate the joy of this occasion, of becoming a son or daughter of the commandment.

RELEVANCE TO THE NEW TESTAMENT

As mentioned previously, the B*ar/Bat Mitzvah* ceremony is not specifically found in the Hebrew Scriptures. However, the rabbinic commentaries contain many references to a ceremony that marks the age of accountability. Surprisingly, the clearest account of an ancient B*ar Mitzvah* ceremony is found in another Jewish book—the New Testament.

> Every year Yeshua's parents went to *Yerushalayim* [Jerusalem] for the festival of Pesach [Passover]. When he was twelve years old, they went up for the festival, as custom required. But after the festival was over,

when his parents returned, Yeshua remained in Yerushalayim. They didn't realize this; supposing that he was somewhere in the caravan, they spent a whole day on the road before they began searching for him among their relatives and friends. Failing to find him, they returned to Yerushalayim to look for him. On the third day they found him—he was sitting in the Temple court among the rabbis, not only listening to them but questioning what they said; and everyone who heard him was astonished at his insight and his responses (Luke 2:41–47).

This Bar Mitzvah ceremony must have been very important for the New Testament writers, since this is the only recorded event of Yeshua's later childhood years. It is no coincidence that it occurred at the age of twelve when, according to tradition, a son became responsible for observing the Jewish feasts. Accordingly, Yosef and Miryam traveled to Jerusalem with their son to celebrate Passover and to prepare him for the duties of becoming a Bar Mitzvah.

However, this Bar Mitzvah turned out to be rather different from the average one. As the family returned by caravan to their home town of Natzeret, they did not at first realize that their son, Yeshua, had remained behind at the Temple. When they finally tracked him down, they found him where any good Bar Mitzvah boy would be—receiving the blessing of the rabbis, as was common in ancient tradition. It caught everyone's attention that this particular student was amazing even the rabbis with the wisdom of his drashah ("teaching") Surely this Bar Mitzvah boy was something special, one who would later proclaim himself to be the Messiah.

While many of the elements of the traditional Bar Mitzvah are visible in this first-century account, this was a Bar Mitzvah to remember. Yeshua is the perfect example of what a Bar Mitzvah should be. As noted in the New Testament:

Even though he was the Son, he learned obedience through his sufferings. And after he had been brought to the goal, he became the source of eternal deliverance to all who obey him (Messianic Jews [Hebrews] 5:8–9).

How amazing it is to realize that Yeshua has been the only perfect Bar Mitzvah in the history of Israel. He has fulfilled all of the Torah on behalf of those who believe in him.

PRACTICAL GUIDE TO A MESSIANIC BAR/BAT MITZVAH CEREMONY

The following is a suggested order of service based on the history of, and the New Covenant understanding of, the Bar/Bat Mitzvah ceremony. Many of these elements are found in the traditional Jewish ceremony. The distinctive of a Messianic ceremony is that it should be reflective of the child's personal commitment to Yeshua. While this ceremony could take place in a home or other building, a Messianic congregation seems to be the most natural expression for this kind of service.

Frequently, Jewish believers wait until the last minute to call their congregational leader regarding their child's Bar/Bat Mitzvah. Although it is commendable that the family has a desire to follow in the tradition of Bar/Bat Mitzvah, such a ceremony is not something to be taken lightly. In addition to being a time of personal commitment, the Bar/Bat Mitzvah ceremony is also a time when a commitment is made to an entire religious community (in this case Messianic). The saying "it takes a whole village to raise a child" is apropos to the meaning of Bar/Bat Mitzvah. The ceremony does not reflect a one-day, or even a one-year, commitment, but is a statement of one's philosophy of life. Accordingly, the family needs to make a commitment, long before the ceremony, to a local congregation. Each family should consult with their local Messianic leader for advice.

The following worship service has worked well at this author's congregation, Kehilat Ariel:

WORSHIP THROUGH MUSIC AND DANCE

WORSHIP THROUGH TRADITIONAL LITURGY
(Fischer and Bronstein, Siddur for Messianic Jews is highly

recommended; see Conclusion for information on how to obtain it)

Introductory Psalms
Barkhu/Sh'ma
Messianic Reading or Reading from the New Covenant
Bar/Bat Mitzvah Ceremony

The child is called to the ark as the Torah service begins. After the appropriate prayers, the Bar/Bat Mitzvah leads the Torah processional through the congregation.

The Torah blessings are chanted.

The Torah portion is chanted. Seven *aliyot* ("goings up" to the *bimah*) are traditional, with the Bar/Bat Mitzvah as the eighth reader. However, it may be simpler if the Bar/Bat Mitzvah is the only reader.

Haftarah blessings are chanted.

The *Haftarah* portion (in the Prophets) is chanted. The number of verses chanted from either the Torah or *Haftarah* should be contingent upon the ability of the child. It is much better to properly chant five verses in Hebrew than to do a sloppy job with fifty verses.

After the *Haftarah* section is chanted, the Bar/Bat Mitzvah delivers his or her *drashah* (short teaching/ speech). During the course of this speech, the child should give a personal testimony of his or her faith in Messiah. This is a great step in fulfilling new religious duties.

SYNAGOGUE PRESENTATIONS

This may include a certificate and other religious gifts from the sabbath school or congregational family. *Mazel tov* and other greetings are expressed at this point.

LEADER'S MESSAGE

It is often an ideal time, especially with the many visitors and guests, to follow up the ceremony with a more expansive message on the theme of the text.

CLOSING PRAYER AND SONG

KIDDUSH

The blessings over the wine and the *challah* (sabbath bread). This can be followed by a special *oneg* (joyful celebration) with refreshments at the congregation or reception hall.

May every believer have a blessed ceremony in the Messiah Yeshua. May all believers show their love for Yeshua by becoming better sons and daughters of his commandments (see John 14:15).

The Jewish Wedding

THE HISTORICAL BACKGROUND

This is what the LORD says: "You say about this place, 'It is a desolate waste, without men or animals.' Yet in the towns of Judah and the streets of Jerusalem that are deserted, inhabited by neither men nor animals, there will be heard once more the sounds of joy and gladness, the voices of bride and bridegroom, and the voices of those who bring thank offerings to the house of the LORD, saying,

'Give thanks to the LORD Almighty,
for the LORD is good;
his love endures forever.'
For I will restore the fortunes of the land as they were
before," says the LORD (Jeremiah 33:10–11).

Of all the customs appointed by God, there is probably none more joyous than that of the Jewish wedding. It is one *simcha* (joyous occasion) that you do not want to miss! Of course, it is joyful enough to just witness the covenant vows between a man and woman who love each other. When you add family and friends, food, music and dance, it is difficult to find a more exuberant celebration.

While a wedding in any culture is a blessing, there are some unique lessons to be learned from the biblical/Jewish wedding ceremony, in particular. The ancient rituals associated with this custom are rich in spiritual truths that remind Israel of their covenant with God and his love for them.

This God-appointed custom can be examined through the three parts spoken of in Jewish tradition.

Shiddukhin

The *shiddukhin* period is the first step in the marriage process and refers to the arrangements preliminary to the legal betrothal. In biblical times, the important first step was the "arrangement." It was common in ancient tradition for the father of the groom to select a bride for his son, sometimes while he was still an infant. Marriage was often looked upon as an expedient family connection or even political alliance; therefore, what would be described as love was often a secondary issue. An excellent illustration of the biblical marriage process is found in the early chapters of the Torah, concerning the life of the patriarch Isaac.

> Abraham was now old and well advanced in years, and the LORD had blessed him in every way. He said to the chief servant in his household, the one in charge of all that he had, "Put your hand under my thigh. I want you to swear by the LORD, the God of heaven and the God of earth, that you will not get a wife for my son from the daughters of the Canaanites, among whom I am living, but will go to my country and my own relatives and get a wife for my son Isaac" (Genesis 24:1–4).

This is a classic example of the *shiddukhin* being initiated for the son of Abraham. Although this was considered the responsibility of the father, many times it was not practical. Therefore, the father could delegate this responsibility by designating a representative. In this case, Abraham sent his servant on a journey to acquire a bride for his son from his own Semitic tribesmen. Throughout the generations, this person was known as the *shadkhan* ("marriage broker" or "matchmaker"). This may sound familiar to anyone who has seen *Fiddler on the Roof.*

Upon meeting the beautiful Rebekah, the servant sent by Abraham clearly saw the hand of God. Convinced of the proper selection, the servant proceeded to the next step of the *shiddukhin*, which is called the *ketubah* ("written"). The *ketubah* includes the provisions and conditions proposed for the marriage. This might be called the original pre-nuptial agreement or, more correctly, the marriage contract. In this Hebrew document, the groom promises to support his wife-to-be, while the bride stipulates the contents of her dowry (financial status). This is highlighted in the account of Abraham's servant, in regard to Rebekah. After talking with Laban (Rebekah's father), the servant reacted in the following way:

> When Abraham's servant heard what they said, he bowed down to the ground before the LORD. Then the servant brought out gold and silver jewelry and articles of clothing and gave them to Rebekah; he also gave costly gifts to her brother and to her mother (Genesis 24:52–53).

Despite the fact that this was an arranged marriage, it seems clear that the consent of the bride was an important contingency clause. This is evidenced when the servant asked Abraham "what if the woman is unwilling to come back with me to this land?" (Genesis 24:5). Fortunately, in Rebekah's case, she agreed to the conditions of the *ketubah* (see Genesis 24:58).

To prepare for the betrothal ceremony, it was common for the bride and groom to separately take a ritual immersion in water (*mikveh*). This ritual immersion in water (*mikveh*) was always symbolic of a spiritual cleansing.

Eyrusin (Betrothal)

After the *mikveh*, the couple appeared under the *huppah* ("canopy") in a public ceremony to express their intention of becoming betrothed, or engaged.

While *eyrusin* means "betrothal," a secondary word often associated with this period is *kiddushin* ("sanctification" or "set-apart"). This secondary term more specifically describes what the betrothal, or engagement period is all about; that is, setting oneself aside for another for the covenant of marriage. *Kiddushin* also refers to the actual *eyrusin* ceremony, which takes place under a *huppah*.

From ancient times, the wedding canopy has been a symbol of a new household being planned (see Psalm 19:5; Joel 2:16). During the ceremony, some items of value were exchanged (e.g., rings) and a cup of wine was shared to seal the *eyrusin* vows.

After this *huppah* ceremony, the couple was considered to be fully entered into the agreement of *eyrusin*. The *eyrusin* period would continue for one year. During this time, the couple was considered married in the modern sense of the word, yet were not allowed to cohabit until the end of the *eyrusin*. Hence, there were no sexual relations at this time and the couple would live in separate dwelling places.

The betrothal period is typified in the story of Isaac, in the gap of time between Rebekah's acceptance and their actual marriage later in Canaan.

The Jewish understanding of *eyrusin* has always been much stronger than our modern understanding of engagement. The *eyrusin* was so binding that the couple would actually need a religious divorce (*get*) in order to annul the contract (see Deuteronomy 24:1–4). The option of a *get* was available only to the husband, as the wife had no say in any divorce proceeding.

Both bride and groom had their respective responsibilities in this betrothal period. The groom was to use this as a time of preparation. As the *huppah* symbolized a new household, so the groom was to focus on preparing a new dwelling place for his bride and, hopefully, children to follow. In biblical times, this was most easily accomplished by simply adding another room to the family's existing home.

As the groom prepared the home during the one-year betrothal period, the bride kept herself busy with her tasks. Specifically, the bride was to focus on her own personal preparation as the wedding day approached. Beautiful wedding garments were to be sewn as a symbol of the joyous occasion to come. More importantly, the bride was to consecrate herself in the true spirit of the betrothal time. For both bride and groom, it was to be a year of introspection and contemplation, readying themselves for this most holy covenant of marriage.

Nissuin (Marriage)

The culminating step in the process of the Jewish wedding ceremony is known as *nissuin*. This is based on the Hebrew verb *nasa*, which literally means "to carry." *Nissuin* was quite a graphic description, as the bride would be waiting for the groom to carry her away to their new home. There was great anticipation as the bride waited for the arrival of her betrothed one. This was to be expected, especially when taking into consideration an element unique to the biblical Jewish wedding; that is, the time of the groom's arrival (and hence the whole wedding party) was to be a surprise. Any bride who took seriously the betrothal period would be expecting the groom at the end of their year-long engagement. However, the exact hour of the ceremony was uncertain, as it was the father of the groom who would give the final approval for the *nissuin* to begin.

The bride and her bridal party would therefore be anxiously watching and waiting for the exact moment. Even in the late evening, the bridal party was to keep their oil lamps burning just in case the wedding was to begin. How would they know when the time had arrived? One custom was for a member of the groom's party to lead the way from the groom's house to the home of the bride, and to shout "Behold, the bridegroom comes!" This would be followed by the sound of the *shofar* (ram's horn), which was used to proclaim Jewish holy days and special events.

At the sound of the *shofar*, the groom would lead a wedding procession through the streets of the village to the house of the bride. The groomsmen would then carry (*nissuin*) the bride back to the groom's house where a *huppah* ("canopy") was once again set up. The couple would once again, as they did one year previous, say a blessing over a cup of wine (a symbol of joy). This cup was clearly distinguished from the previous cup, as is reflected in the traditional *sheva b'rakhot* ("seven blessings") that accompany it. This second stage of the *huppah* ceremony, as found in the *nissuin* custom, serves as the finalization of the earlier promises and vows. What was promised in the *eyrusin* ceremony was now consummated in the *nissuin* ceremony. For the first time, the couple was free to consummate their marriage by having sexual relations and by living together as husband and wife (see Genesis 24:66–67).

The pinnacle of this joyful celebration was the marriage supper. This was more than just a sit-down dinner for all the guests, but included seven full days of food, music, dance and celebration (see Judges 14:10–12). After all the wonderful festivities, the new husband was free to bring his wife to their new home and to live together within the full covenant of marriage.

TRADITIONAL JEWISH OBSERVANCE

Since the days of Abraham, this has been the structure of the Jewish wedding ceremony. Many of these basic customs are still included in the modern Jewish observance. Whether it is a wedding in Jerusalem, London or San Diego, it is easy to recognize the common thread of connection back to the Torah. Actually, many of these biblical elements and traditions are found in other non-Jewish wedding ceremonies around the world.

The modern observance of the wedding ceremony has evolved over the years to include some interesting additions. Each aspect is meant to remind us of some element of spiritual truth important to Jewish history or culture. The most noticeable change in the modern Jewish ceremony is that there is no longer a gap of time between the *eyrusin* ceremony and the *nissuin*. Some scholars track this change back to the Middle Ages where, because of the perilous dangers to the Jewish community, there was no guarantee that both bride and groom would survive the one-year time gap. Hence, the two separate parts of the *huppah* ceremony were combined into one with much of the same symbolism, illustrating both the *eyrusin* and *nissuin*.

Today, a fairly standard structure for the Jewish wedding includes the *eyrusin* and *nissuin*. In keeping with the symbolism of the *eyrusin*, the first part of the ceremony actually takes place before the main body of the wedding. This is the signing of the *ketubah*, which usually happens just minutes before the processional. The modern *ketubah* adheres to the ancient Hebrew and Aramaic formula, although the English translations may vary. In Orthodox Jewish circles (especially within the land of Israel), the *ketubah* is considered a binding legal document that may even be submitted as court evidence. However, most Jewish weddings take place outside Israel, where the *ketubah* is strictly a symbolic, albeit important, custom. The binding document in such cases is the marriage license issued by the local government.

In a private room with the rabbi and at least two witnesses, the bride and the groom sign the *ketubah*. In comparison, it is usually taboo for the groom to see the bride before the "Christian" wedding ceremony. However, at the Jewish ceremony, it is actually a requirement for the groom to see his bride before the *ketubah* is signed. Why is this? A Jewish groom by the name of Jacob did not properly check under the veil of his bride and actually ended up with the wrong woman (see Genesis 29:25). It seems that future Jewish grooms have learned from this sad lesson and make sure that they have the right bride!

While some ancient Jewish communities might adhere to some of the early cultural practices, most communities start the actual wedding ceremony with a simple processional. It is noteworthy that some groups (e.g., those from Iran and Yemen) have continued the custom of pre-arranged marriages. After the signing of the *ketubah*, the *huppah* is assembled at the wedding site. This could be either a free-standing canopy with support bases or a canopy with four hand-held poles. The *huppah* roof might be made of special embroidered fabric or a traditional prayer shawl. This is the focal point to which the wedding processional marches. The first in line might be the rabbi, followed by the various groomsmen and bridesmaids. Everyone takes their proper positions. The rabbi is under the center of the *huppah* with the wedding party normally stationed on each side of the canopy.

This processional represents the ancient tradition of the groom retrieving his bride from her house. Before the groom begins his march, the rabbi says:

Barukh habah b'shem Adonai.
Blessed is he who comes in the name of the Lord.

At this point, the groom is led by his parents until they are in front of the *huppah*. A curious fact is that the groom lines up on the right side as he faces the rabbi. This is the opposite of most "Christian" weddings, where the men line up on the left side. It is difficult to know if the non-Jewish community made the change or if the Jewish community did so as a statement of their distinctiveness.

All eyes are looking up the aisle as the bride appears, with her parents escorting her. The rabbi says:

B'rukhah haba'ah b'shem Adonai.

Blessed is she who comes in the name of the Lord.

The bride makes her grand appearance, walking majestically towards her betrothed. As they meet in front of the *huppah*, the bride may follow the traditional custom of circling the groom three times. As this is transpiring, the rabbi explains that this is symbolic of the three-fold betrothal that is mentioned in Scripture. As God spoke to Israel through the prophet Hosea, "I will betroth you to me forever, . . . in righteousness . . . in love and compassion. I will betroth you in faithfulness . . ." (Hosea 2:19–20). The couple join arm-in-arm as bride and groom under the *huppah*.

The rabbi begins his address to the couple with their family and friends as witnesses. Hebrew blessings may be recounted or other introductory statements made concerning the importance of the occasion. The central point is often a *drashah* ("sermon") highlighting the spiritual values of marriage.

The *drashah*, regardless how long it may be, is followed by the first cup of wine. This cup is symbolic of the intent to enter into the *eyrusin* (i.e., engagement) part of the marriage covenant. Having understood the stipulations of the *ketubah* (i.e., contract), the couple seals the first part of the agreement with a sip of wine under the *huppah*. The rabbi chants the traditional blessing:

Barukh atah Adonai, eloheynu melekh ha'olam, borey p'ri ha'gafen. Amen.

Blessed art Thou, O Lord our God, King of the universe, who creates the fruit of the vine. Amen.

The following is added, in Hebrew and English:

> Blessed art Thou, O Lord our God, King of the
> universe, who has sanctified us by his commandments
> and commanded us concerning forbidden unions; who
> has forbidden us those who are merely betrothed, and
> permitted us those who are married to us through *huppah*
> and the sacred covenant of marriage. Blessed art Thou,
> O Lord who sanctifies Thy people Israel through *huppah*
> and the sacred covenant of marriage. Amen.

As the wine cup is drunk by the bride and groom, they symbolically enter into the full *eyrusin* contract. In contrast to the ancient ceremony, the modern wedding structure moves immediately to the *nissuin* section. Most couples find it a great encouragement that the year-long engagement has been condensed into the same *huppah* ceremony. Nonetheless, the two distinctive parts of the Jewish wedding are still clearly seen.

The ceremony segues into the vows that are exchanged between the bride and groom. This may be a combination of the traditional Hebrew vow as well as a personal statement in English. It is at this point that the symbols of the vows are brought forth, customarily gold rings. Some traditional groups believe that it is too ostentatious to have any gems, so they prefer simple metal bands. Since the Talmud speaks of the man acquiring a wife, it is the groom alone who says the traditional vow. As he places the ring on the finger of his bride, the groom says:

> *Harey at m'kudeshet li, b'taba'at zu, k'dat Moshe v'Yisraeyl.*
> With this ring you are wed to me, in accordance with
> the Law of Moses and of Israel.

Since there have been vows exchanged publicly before witnesses and rings have been exchanged, the rabbi can make the declaration that this couple is now officially husband and wife. However, there are still some significant elements needed for the completion of the *nissuin*.

There is usually a public reading of the *ketubah*. Then the second cup of wine is filled for the *sheva b'rakhot* ("seven blessings"). This beautiful Hebrew melody praises God for many of his blessings, including the creation of man and woman, the peace of Jerusalem and the joy of the marriage covenant. At the end of this moving prayer, the couple drinks from the cup to symbolize the completion of the *nissuin* (marriage) ceremony.

However, there still remains the well-known custom that developed in later years—the breaking of the glass. It is said

that this custom was started by one of the rabbis of the talmudic age who, upon observing all the joy of the wedding feast, suddenly threw down a glass goblet. His point was that even in times of great joy, one can never forget the suffering of Jerusalem and the destruction of the Temple (*Babylonian Talmud*, Berakhot 31a). In the modern ceremony, the breaking of the glass occurs at the very end of the wedding. It is a bittersweet reminder of the seriousness of life; yet, as the glass is crushed by the groom's heel, a jubilant cry of *mazel tov* ("congratulations") rings throughout the crowd. After a kiss between the new husband and wife, they joyously walk up the aisle to the sounds of celebratory music. This is followed by the marriage supper and reception, with food, music and dance. What a *simcha* (joyous occasion)!

RELEVANCE TO THE NEW TESTAMENT

There are many customs appointed by God as teaching tools. The Jewish wedding ceremony might just be the richest of them all, with many spiritual lessons interwoven within it. In addition, many of the elements of the wedding ceremony were meant to point to the goal of all the Scriptures, namely Messiah Yeshua (Galatians 3:24).

In a unique way, the Jewish wedding ceremony (as opposed to any other cultural expression) is a detailed illustration of the Messiah's relationship with his followers. It is no wonder, therefore, that there are numerous references in the New Testament Scriptures to the importance of this lifecycle event. These references will now be examined by using the outline of the Jewish ceremony, beginning with the *shiddukhin* period.

Shiddukhin
The *shiddukhin* starts with the selection of the bride; so, too, believers in Yeshua have been chosen as Messiah's bride (see Ephesians 1:4). It is the father of the groom or, in some cases, a designated *shadkhan* ("matchmaker") who does the selection.

Saul of Tarsus (Paul), a Pharisee who became a believer in Yeshua, made the following observation about the spiritual significance of *shiddukhin*:

I would like you to bear with me in a little foolishness—please do bear with me! For I am jealous for you with God's kind of jealousy; since I promised to present you as a pure virgin in marriage to your one husband, the Messiah (2 Corinthians 11:1–2).

In this passage, Saul exhorted the believers of Corinth to stay on track with their faith, by making a comparison with the *shiddukhin*. Saul compared himself to a spiritual *shadkhan* who introduced (or presented) these believers to their prospective husband (i.e., Yeshua the Messiah).

During the *shiddukhin*, a price is specified through the *ketubah*. This contract specifies the conditions and provisions for the upcoming wedding, for both bride and groom. In biblical times, part of the bride's dowry might include a headband of coins that was worn during the ceremony (Gower, *The New Manners and Customs of Bible Times*, p. 64). Since this headband of coins represented part of the marriage contract, the loss of any of these coins would cause great worry (see Luke 15:8–10).

In the larger picture, a believer's spiritual *ketubah* is none other than the New Covenant itself. The groom (i.e., the Messiah) promises to pay a proper price (i.e., his own death) for his beloved. Meanwhile, the bride (i.e., the body of Messianic believers) promises to pay her dowry with her own yielded life. As Saul beautifully summed up in his letter to the Corinthians: "For you were bought at a price. So use your bodies to glorify God" (1 Corinthians 6:20).

Eyrusin (Betrothal)

The *eyrusin* ceremony (*kiddushin*) includes the blessing of the first cup under the *huppah*. One of the last acts of Yeshua while he was in his earthly body was to bless the cup representing the New Covenant. He stated that he would not taste another cup with his disciples until a later time in the kingdom of God (see Matthew 26:27–29). What perfect symbolism connected with the *eyrusin*, the betrothal time!

There is theological debate concerning the eternal security of the believer, the possibility that one may lose his or her salvation. The lessons of the *eyrusin* contribute to resolving this discussion.

Now that the two parties have agreed to partake of the *eyrusin* blessings under the *huppah*, they are as good as married. True, they are not to live together yet, but the promise is so sure that it would take a religious divorce (*get*) to nullify the contract. In addition, the *get* is an option available only to the husband. The lesson is clear from the Jewish wedding: true believers are eternally secure in Messiah's covenant, because we cannot break it and he says he never will. As Yeshua said, ". . . I give them eternal life. They will absolutely never be destroyed, and no one will snatch them from my hands" (John 10:28). It is an incredible blessing to know that those who believe in Yeshua the Messiah have entered with him into the engagement period according to the Jewish understanding, as defined by the *eyrusin* period!

Since believers in Yeshua have consented to the conditions of the *eyrusin*, they enter into the betrothal period. This is the period of time (biblically, one year) between the solemn first cup of the *eyrusin* ceremony and the full marriage as symbolized in the second cup. Although the couple is considered married in a legal sense, they are not to live together as husband and wife. There is too much that still needs to be done. The groom has his own responsibilities, the most pressing one being the preparing of their future home. In the ancient Middle East, this was most likely to take the form of adding a room to the family's existing home.

The preparation of a future home fits with the teaching of Yeshua. The Messiah was trying to comfort his disciples concerning his impending death and departure from the earth. As troubling as this was to those followers, there was great hope expressed when Yeshua said:

> Don't let yourselves be disturbed. Trust in God and trust in me. In my Father's house are many places to live. If there weren't, I would have told you; because I am going there to prepare a place for you. Since I am going and preparing a place for you, I will return to take you with me; so that where I am, you may be also (John 14:1–3).

Yeshua, our heavenly bridegroom, has taken the first vows with his New Covenant bride; that is, Jews and Gentiles who call on his name. He is now fulfilling his responsibility of preparing a special home for his wife-to-be. It is understandable that the immediate reaction of the disciples to Yeshua's death would be one of fear and doubt. However, in God's wisdom, this temporary separation from the groom perfectly fulfills the purpose of the betrothal period. It must have been a comfort to those disciples to realize that their redeemer and Messiah was simply completing the spiritual plan of the Father, as seen in the betrothal.

The bride also had her preparations. During the one-year betrothal period, she consecrated herself by her pure life and prepared holy garments for the upcoming marriage. She entered the *mikveh* (i.e., ritual water immersion) immediately before the marriage as a symbol of moral cleansing. In terms of eschatology, the spiritual application is clear. Believers in Yeshua, as his espoused bride, are to consecrate themselves and to keep their spiritual lives pure in preparation for the second cup. Saul amplified this truth in his letter to the believers in Ephesus:

> As for husbands, love your wives, just as the Messiah loved the Messianic Community, indeed, gave himself up on its behalf, in order to set it apart for God, making it clean through immersion in the mikveh, so to speak, in order to present the Messianic Community to himself as a bride to be proud of, without a spot, wrinkle or any such thing, but holy and without defect (Ephesians 5:25–27).

The last two thousand years have been the betrothal period between the Messiah and his bride. As with any anxious bride, the wait has at times been difficult. Yet, the bridegroom is ready to return. Believers in Yeshua need to ask themselves if they are keeping their garments clean and keeping their *ketubah* promises.

Nissuin

The *nissuin* completes the spiritual picture. According to ancient biblical tradition, the groom would come for his bride at the end of the one-year *eyrusin*. Everything is made ready and the bride anxiously awaits his arrival. The groom could only come for his bride after the father had given the command. With the groom leading a procession through the streets of the village, the *shofar* would be sounded to the shouts of "the bridegroom comes!"

The *nissuin* tradition must have been on the mind of Saul as he wrote to those with questions about Yeshua's return:

> For the Lord himself will come down from heaven with a rousing cry, with a call from one of the ruling angels, and with God's shofar; those who died united with the Messiah will be the first to rise; then we who are left still alive will be caught up with them in the clouds to meet the Lord in the air; and thus we will always be with the Lord. So encourage each other with these words (1 Thessalonians 4:16–18).

This prophetic event, commonly called the "rapture" (the catching up of believers), is perfectly illustrated within the Jewish wedding ceremony. As those betrothed to Yeshua, his followers await the start of the second part of the *huppah* tradition. The *sheva b'rakhot* ("seven blessings") mark the completion of the marriage.

At the close of the *nissuin*, there will be a jubilant celebration. At the end of the wedding feast, the Messiah will return to Jerusalem with his bride and establish his one-thousand year earthly kingdom (see Revelation 20:4). The wedding party will continue in Jerusalem, as the rest of the resurrected believers from every age will join in the festivities. What a reception that will be! Believers in Yeshua will dwell with the Messiah as spiritual husband and wife.

While there is considerable theological debate about the timing of the *nissuin* events, one thing is certain: everyone should choose to RSVP to God's invitation. As the apostle John saw the heavenly vision of the *huppah* ceremony to come, he heard the redeemed multitude saying:

Let us rejoice and be glad! Let us give him the glory! For the time has come for the wedding of the Lamb, and his Bride has prepared herself—fine linen, bright and clean has been given her to wear.

("Fine linen" means the righteous deeds of God's people.)

And the angel said to me, "Write: 'How blessed are those who have been invited to the wedding feast of the Lamb'" (Revelation 19:7–9)!

The redeemed from all of history (i.e., Jew and Gentile who have responded to God's way of salvation) will dwell with our God for eternity. The Jewish wedding ceremony is God's appointed custom to remind believers in Yeshua of the great things to come in Messiah's kingdom.

All people need to answer the question of whether or not they trust in the death and resurrection of Messiah for their salvation. Only believers in Yeshua have been invited to this Jewish wedding ceremony. May the groom, Yeshua, come soon to start the celebration.

PRACTICAL GUIDE FOR A MESSIANIC WEDDING CEREMONY

Preparing for a Messianic wedding requires addressing certain issues. A ceremony like this makes it clear that the non-Jewish spouse has a Jewish heart, affirming the Jewish perspective of the faith. Therefore, it is not a major issue if one of the spouses is not Jewish. However, in cases where either one of the spouses is not a believer in Yeshua, the wedding should not be performed (based on 2 Corinthians 6:14). To confirm that the marriage is in the will of God, pre-marital counseling should be mandatory. An engaged couple should consult with the local Messianic leader concerning this important preparation time.

The following suggested order of service is based on the wedding customs of biblical times and their modern adaptations. As with many of the traditions and customs, one should adapt this ceremony to fit the personal convictions and desires of the bride and groom. Above all, may the distinctiveness of their faith in Yeshua be clearly seen in this beautiful ceremony.

In setting up for the ceremony, the following supplies will be needed:

1. Kiddush cup for wine
2. Kosher wine or grape juice in a bottle
3. A glass for breaking, wrapped in a cloth napkin
4. Ketubah
5. Huppah
6. White kippot (skullcaps) for the men

The order of service is as follows:

SIGNING OF THE KETUBAH

This document is to be signed by both bride and groom before the start of the main ceremony. Likewise, the Messianic leader and two witnesses (usually the maid of honor and best man) are to sign it. A small group of family and friends may be invited to watch the signing. For the actual ketubah, a Messianic one is recommended (see the Conclusion for information on how to obtain one); however, a traditional ketubah or a customized one may be drawn up if desired.

MUSIC PRELUDE

This can include any appropriate instrumental or vocal music that the bride and groom desire.

PROCESSIONAL

Normally, the Messianic leader will take his place under the back part of the huppah (which should be an elevated platform), followed by the groomsmen and bridal party. The men line up on the left side of the huppah as the audience faces it; the women are on the right side.

INVOCATION FOR THE GROOM

When the groom begins his march, the Messianic leader shall say:

Barukh habah b'shem Adonai.
Blessed is he who comes in the name of the Lord.

The groom is escorted by his parents to the front of the *huppah*. After giving them a farewell kiss or hug, the parents are seated while the groom remains standing at the *huppah*, looking back up the aisle.

INVOCATION FOR THE BRIDE
Before the bride begins her march, the Messianic leader shall say:

B'rukhah haba'a b'shem Adonai..
Blessed is she who comes in the name of the Lord.

(The groom may read Proverbs 31:10–12 as the bride begins her march down the aisle.)
The bride is led by her parents until she is in front of the *huppah*, facing the groom. At this point, the bride may circle the groom three times as the Messianic leader reads and explains the passage from Hosea 2:19.

As the bride finishes the circling, she joins arms with the groom as they both step under the *huppah*. They face the Messianic leader who says:

Mi adir al hakol. Mi barukh al hakol. Mi gadol al hakol. Hu y'vareykh et he'khatan v'et ha'kalah.

He who is supremely mighty; He who is supremely praised; He who is supremely great—May He bless this bridegroom and bride.

THE MESSIANIC LEADER'S ADDRESS
Since most Messianic weddings are attended by a diverse crowd, including many non-Messianic Jewish friends, this is an opportune time for the Messianic leader to make some appropriate introductory remarks. It is most helpful and important to clarify that this is a Messianic ceremony and exactly what that means. Many of the customs will be familiar

to Jewish guests; however, the wedding couple has also chosen to express the New Covenant connection, since this is an expression of their personal faith in Yeshua the Messiah. In the case of mixed marriages (i.e., Jewish and non-Jewish believers), it can be a beautiful testimony to explain that the Gentile spouse also loves the biblical/Jewish customs because they are consistent with his or her faith.

After the Messianic leader's introductory remarks, an opening personal prayer may be offered to ask God's blessing on this joyous occasion. This is followed by a short sermon that addresses some issues related to marriage. It is a perfect time to incorporate any preferred verses from the Scriptures.

The *Eyrusin* Cup

The best man fills the first cup of wine and the Messianic leader says:

> *Barukh atah Adonai, eloheynu melekh ha'olam, borey p'ri ha'gafen. Amen.*
> Blessed art Thou, O Lord our God, King of the universe who creates the fruit of the vine. Amen.

(The additional longer blessing may be used if desired. See above.)

The best man gives the first cup of wine to the groom who takes a taste and gives his bride a taste.

THE VOWS

At this time, the Messianic leader says:

> [*Names of groom and bride*] will now exchange the traditional wedding vows. By so doing, they will be openly committing themselves to each other; to share the same joys, the same sorrows, and whatever God may bring in their lives together.

There are basically three options for the ceremony; traditional English vows, personalized English vows; and the traditional Hebrew vow. The traditional English vows are read by the Messianic leader, first to the groom:

> [Name of groom], do you of your own free will and consent take this woman [name of bride] to be your wedded wife from this day forward, for better, for worse, for richer, for poorer, in sickness and in health, to live together after God's holy commandment? Will you love her, comfort her, honor her, cherish her, and keep her; and forsaking all others, cleave only to her, as long as you both shall live?

The groom says: "I do."

The Messianic leader says to the bride:

> [Name of bride], do you of your own free will and consent take this man [name of groom] to be your wedded husband from this day forward, for better, for worse, for richer, for poorer, in sickness and in health, to live together after God's holy commandment? Will you love him, honor him, inspire him, cherish him, and keep him; and forsaking all others, cleave only to him, as long as you both shall live?

The bride says: "I do."

The Messianic leader asks, "What symbols do you have of these vows?" The ring-bearer(s) gives the rings to the Messianic leader, who says:

> From earliest times the ring has been a symbol of wedded love. It is made of pure gold to symbolize pure love. Being one unbroken circle, it symbolizes unending love. As often as either of you sees these golden circles, may you be reminded of this important moment and the unending love you promise.

The Messianic leader leads the groom in saying the Hebrew blessing as the groom places the ring on the bride's ring finger:

Harey at m'kudeshet li b'taba'at zu k'dat Moshe v'Yisraeyl.

With this ring you are wed to me in accordance with the Law of Moses and of Israel.

If so desired, a Messianic phrase may be added at the end of each sentence:

. . . b'shem Ha'Av, Yeshua Ha'Mashiakh, v'Ruakh Ha'Kodesh.

. . . in the name of the Father, Yeshua the Messiah, and the Holy Spirit.

In Jewish tradition, the man is the only one who is required to say the blessing over the ring. However, the woman is often allowed to say the same English blessing for her part of the ceremony.

The Messianic leader now proclaims:

Since you have promised your love to each other before God and these witnesses, and exchanged these symbols of genuine love, I hereby announce, by virtue of the authority vested in me, that you are now husband and wife, so to live together until death do you part. What therefore God has joined together, let no man separate.

At this moment in the ceremony, a special musical number is often included to help everyone reflect on the meaning of the occasion.

READING OF THE KETUBAH

The Messianic leader can explain the symbolism of the ketubah and can actually read the text as a declaration of the values of this newly wedded couple.

THE NISSUIN CUP

The best man fills the second cup of wine. The Messianic leader explains the spiritual symbolism associated with this custom, especially in light of faith in the Messiah. The Messianic leader chants the *sheva b'rakhot* ("seven blessings") in Hebrew (refer to Scherman, *The Rabbinical Council of America Edition of The Artscroll Siddur*—see the bibliography—or to any other traditional *siddur*). After the Hebrew is chanted, the Messianic leader reads the English translation:

1. Blessed art Thou, O Lord our God, King of the universe, who has created all things for Thy glory. Amen.

2. Blessed art Thou, O Lord our God, King of the universe, creator of man. Amen.

3. Blessed art Thou, O Lord our God, King of the universe, who has made man in thine image, after thy likeness, and has prepared for him, out of his very self, an eternal soul. Blessed art Thou, O Lord, creator of man. Amen.

4. May Zion who was barren be exceedingly glad and exult, when her children are gathered within her in joy. Blessed art Thou, O Lord, who makes Zion joyful through her children. Amen.

5. O make these loved companions greatly to rejoice, even as of old Thou didst gladden thy creatures in the garden of Eden. Blessed art Thou, O Lord, who makes bridegroom and bride to rejoice. Amen.

6. Blessed art Thou, O Lord our God, King of the universe, who has created joy and gladness, bridegroom and bride, mirth and exultation, pleasure and delight, love, brotherhood, peace and fellowship. Soon may there be heard in the cities of Judah, and in the streets of Jerusalem, the voice of joy and gladness, the voice of the bridegroom and the voice of the bride, the jubilant voice of bridegrooms from their canopies, and of youths from their feasts of songs. Blessed art

Thou, O Lord, who makes the bridegroom to rejoice with the bride. Amen.

7.   Blessed art Thou, O Lord our God, King of the universe, who creates the fruit of the vine. Amen.

The best man gives the groom the wine cup as he and the bride take a sip.

CONCLUSION

The Messianic leader should give a brief explanation of the custom of breaking the glass. It might be good to also alert the crowd to the traditional shout of "Mazel Tov," which comes immediately after the groom crushes the glass. At the proper moment, the groom is exhorted to break the glass. The groom and bride may kiss, and it is fitting that the Messianic leader concludes the service with a moment of personal prayer over the couple.

At the end of the prayer, the couple faces the audience and the Messianic leader says "It is my privilege to present to you Mr. and Mrs. [name]." At that time, the music will often start playing the joyful sounds of traditional wedding songs (a common one is Od Yishama, from Jeremiah 33). The bridesmaids and groomsmen march down the aisle in a recessional in the opposite order from which they entered.

It is now time for the reception which, in good Jewish fashion, should be a simcha (celebration)! Mazel Tov! May the beautiful customs of the Jewish wedding always remind believers in Yeshua of their soon coming groom, Yeshua the Messiah.

5

Death and Mourning

> The Lord is my shepherd, I shall not be in want.
> He makes me lie down in green pastures,
> he leads me beside quiet waters,
> he restores my soul.
> He guides me in paths of righteousness
> for his name's sake.
> Even though I walk
> through the valley of the shadow of death,
> I will fear no evil,
> for you are with me;
> your rod and your staff,
> they comfort me.
> You prepare a table before me

in the presence of my enemies.
You anoint my head with oil;
my cup overflows.
Surely goodness and love will follow me
all the days of my life,
and I will dwell in the house of the LORD
forever (Psalm 23).

Death has been mankind's greatest enemy throughout history. The statistics are pretty overwhelming; every single person will face death! Despite this bleak reality, this generation seems to be in a state of denial regarding its own mortality. There are health clubs, fad diets and new age philosophies that testify to this truth. Of course, this is not the first generation to try to turn back the course of the inevitable.

History is strewn with the evidence of mankind's battle with this archenemy. The Egyptians stored up their riches in the pyramids so that the journey would be pleasant to the next world. Hindus chose to believe that death is just another cycle in the wheel of unending life through reincarnation.

The Jewish approach to death is starkly realistic in comparison to the many world views that have existed throughout history. The Jewish approach does not allow one to deny or escape the reality of death. Death is a certainty and, even in tragic situations, a part of life that is ordained by God.

The first book of the Torah described death as a part of the judgment associated with the spiritual fall of mankind. After Adam and Eve failed their test of moral obedience in the Garden of Eden, certain new conditions prevailed in the world. Among them, God said:

By the sweat of your brow
you will eat your food
until you return to the ground,
since from it you were taken;
for dust you are
and to dust you will return
(Genesis 3:19).

The man (*adam*) was taken from the dust (*adamah*). This play on words in the Torah reflects the spiritual truth of mankind's dilemma. Disobedience and sin have brought physical death—a return to dust (*adamah*). The separation of the body from the soul ended man's fleshly existence on earth.

However, the Jewish perspective always held out hope for a better life and for the world to come. Although the body is under the curse of physical death, the rabbis believed that every Jew would be resurrected and experience a spiritual entity. As the writer of *Kohelet* (Ecclesiastes) reflected on death, he noted that "the dust returns to the ground it came from, and the spirit returns to God who gave it" (Ecclesiastes 12:7).

The manner in which this process takes place has always been a mystery to the sages. Rabbi Joshua *ben Chananiah* summarized the common sentiment: "When they come to life again, we will consult about the matter" (*Babylonian Talmud*, Niddah 70b)! However, there seems to be a consensus as to the reality of the resurrection of the dead. There are many biblical verses that led the rabbinic commentators to this conclusion. They were also led to the conclusion that there was a judgment to come, and that this judgment would determine whether mankind would spend eternity in blessing or in condemnation. The doctrines of *olam habah* ("the world to come") and the coming judgment unfold progressively in the later writings of the *Tanakh* (Hebrew Scriptures). The Book of Daniel provides an account of what will transpire in the last times for Israel:

> At that time Michael, the great prince who protects your people, will arise. There will be a time of distress such as has not happened from the beginning of nations until then. But at that time your people— everyone whose name is found written in the book— will be delivered. Multitudes who sleep in the dust of the earth will awake: some to everlasting life, others to shame and everlasting contempt (Daniel 12:1–2).

The rabbis believed that upon death a person's body would return to the earth. However, as the body patiently awaited the future resurrection, the spirit would descend to a place called *Sheol*. This spiritual abode is said to consist of two different compartments: a place of blessing, called *Paradise*, and a place of judgment, called *Geyhinnom*. The latter was considered a terrible destiny, as is seen in the background of the Hebrew name. *Gey-Hinnom* literally means "Valley of Hinnom," which is one of the ravines surrounding the city of Jerusalem. The startling thing about this place is that it often served as a place of pagan (even human) sacrifice and a burning garbage dump. For a Jew in ancient Jerusalem, the name of *Geyhinnom* conjured up the most horrid picture imaginable. It was certainly an apt description for the spiritual place of judgment. The Greeks later called the place *Gehenna* or, as translated in English, Hell. This judgment was so terrible that the talmudic rabbis believed that a faithful Jew would be spared its anguish: "All Israel has a share in the world to come" (*Jerusalem Talmud*, Sanhedrin 11:1).

So strongly did rabbinic theology adhere to the concepts of the world to come and future judgment that Maimonides (the *Rambam*) included this statement as a part of his Thirteen Principles of the Jewish Faith:

> I believe with perfect faith that there will be a resurrec-tion of the dead at the time when it shall please the Creator, blessed be his name, and exalted be the remembrance of him forever and ever (thirteenth Principle as translated by Philips, *Daily Prayers*, p. 167).

Historically, the Jewish people have believed in the resur-rection of the dead. It is unfortunate that many contemporary Jews, including entire liberal branches (e.g., Reform Judaism), have either ignored or disavowed this central doctrine. Con-sequently, there are many modern Jews who have no concept of the world to come or simply reject it outright. Modern Judaism tends to focus on the importance of the here and now, which certainly is significant. However, the hope and centrality of *olam habah* need to be restored as a central teaching in Judaism today.

This hope of the resurrection and the world to come was a driving force among many of the biblical forefathers. Of all the examples in Scripture, perhaps the most amazing is the testimony of Job, who suffered such incredible losses in his life. As he reflected on his almost hopeless situation, Job revealed his true faith in something beyond this life:

I know that my Redeemer lives,
and that in the end he will stand upon the earth.
And after my skin has been destroyed,
yet in my flesh I will see God
(Job 19:25–26).

As important as this earthly life is, there has always been a larger, grander hope of eternity revealed in the Scriptures. God will correct all injustices and heal all the problems of this short life. When properly understood, the reality of death and the judgment to come should lead one to have the same attitude as reflected in the prayer of Moses: "Teach us to number our days aright, that we may gain a heart of wisdom" (Psalm 90:12).

TRADITIONAL JEWISH OBSERVANCE

Although there is considerable neglect of the teaching of *olam habah* today, the Jewish community retains many of its truths in the customs associated with death and mourning. Many of these traditions are a direct application of God's appointed customs. Many spiritual values can be seen and learned as one understands the traditional Jewish way of coping with this final stage of the biblical lifecycle.

Within the Jewish customs, one finds a common theme of respect for life and for those touched by death. The body is considered the vessel of the spirit that is given by God (see Proverbs 20:27). Therefore, it is important that proper care and honor be accorded to the burial of the departed. It is just as important that the grief and spiritual state of the mourners be properly attended. The modern burial customs speak much about these concerns for the dead as well as the living.

In Orthodox tradition, interment must be completed as soon as possible after death. Since the Bible places great emphasis on respecting blood, the process of embalming (which involves removing the blood) is not normally permitted. For the same reason, autopsies are not performed unless another life can be saved by it, or civil law requires it. According to rabbinic interpretation, cremation is not an option, as this would violate the command to bury the dead in the earth (see Genesis 3:19). With these restrictions, it is easy to see why a traditional Jewish burial often takes place within 24 hours of death. The only exceptions would be because of the Sabbath or to allow travel time for relatives to attend the funeral.

The preparation of the body for burial is considered one of the more important *mitzvot* ("commandments" or "good deeds"). Although there is no embalming, there is a great deal of work that is done regarding the proper washing and cleansing of the body. The body is clothed with a white robe or shroud, called the *takhrikhim*. This garment is modeled after the priestly garments worn in the Temple. One peculiarity is that the garments have no pockets, which accentuates the fact that one leaves this world without any worldly possessions. If the deceased is a male, his *tallit* (prayer shawl) is draped over him with the fringes (*tzitziyot*) cut. This demonstrates that his earthly call to keep the commandments is no longer binding. During this process, the body is never left alone, but is watched during the *shmirah* (the "watching vigil"). Traditional Jews normally form a religious burial society, *Chevra Kaddisha* ("Holy Society"), that performs these services. Even though the customs may vary concerning burial dress, the symbolism of the simple shroud is striking. The rabbis encouraged simplicity as a way of keeping a proper perspective. Whether a cab driver or the President of Israel, all people are equal in death (Lamm, *The Jewish Way in Death and Mourning*, p. 239).

The same can be said in regard to the casket. In contrast to the prevailing worldly view, the Jewish emphasis is on simplicity. While some people of the world opt to be buried in elaborate caskets, the Jewish tradition says that a simple wood casket is ideal. It becomes abundantly clear that the Jewish philosophy also addresses some practical problems often facing the mourners. It is unfortunate that many times a grieving family, out of love or even guilt, will choose to invest a great sum of money in the funeral arrangements. Many people would welcome a guiding principle. In Jewish tradition it is already settled. Simplicity is a *mitzvah* because we are all equal in death.

The funeral itself presents a number of notable spiritual lessons. In keeping with the theme of respect, the normative practice is not to have an open casket. Similarly, it is usually considered out of character to have flower displays or even music at an Orthodox Jewish funeral. Such things are symbolic of the joys and pleasures of this life and are forbidden at such an occasion. However, it is the opinion of this author that it is acceptable to incorporate special music, as King David did on various occasions, to express one's faith and hope in God.

Before the start of the memorial service, the immediate members of the family follow the ritual of *kria* ("tearing"). As was done in biblical times, the family rends a part of their clothing, normally on the left side by the heart, as a sign of mourning (see Genesis 37:34). The funeral home usually provides black ribbons that can be substituted for the clothing. This custom of *kria* is observed for the first seven days of the mourning period. When the garment is torn, the following blessing is said by the mourners:

Barukh atah Adonai, eloheynu melekh ha'olam dayan ha'emet. Amen.

Blessed art Thou, O Lord our God, King of the universe, the true Judge. Amen.

The rabbi or cantor leads the service, which includes various Hebrew prayers, Psalms and English readings. Among these is the ancient *El Moley Rakhamim*, which is chanted in Hebrew and is translated as follows:

O God, full of compassion, Thou who dwellest in high!
Grant perfect rest unto the soul of _____,
who has departed from this world. Lord of mercy,
bring him/her into Thy presence and let his/her soul
be bound up in the bond of eternal life. Be Thou his/
her possession, and may his/her repose be peace.
Amen (Central Conference of American Rabbis, *Rabbi's
Manual*, p. 71).

The funeral includes a eulogy, which serves as a reminder
of the deceased and his or her work in the community.

At the grave site, it is a requirement to have at least ten
men (a *minyan*) gathered for the recitation of the *Kaddish*. This
ancient prayer, written in Aramaic, is usually the most well
known custom associated with the Jewish funeral. Some
people, therefore, mistakenly believe that it is a prayer for the
dead. Ironically, the *Kaddish* does not even mention death, but
is a powerful prayer exalting God and seeking the establish-
ment of his kingdom. It teaches the lesson that each person
needs to affirm God's sovereignty and plan for his or her life,
even during a time of great sorrow.

It is customary, as an act of love and grief, for each family
member to take turns shoveling some dirt on the lowered
casket. Normally, there will be no grave marker until the special
unveiling service at the one-year anniversary of the death.

After the funeral and graveside service, the immediate
family (i.e., spouse, parents, children and siblings) enters
into three periods of mourning. Based on Genesis 50:10, the
first segment is called *shiva* ("seven"), consisting of seven days
starting at the conclusion of the funeral. The family starts this
time of intense mourning by following a number of important
customs. The *kria* clothing or ribbons are still worn, and
shaving and make-up are prohibited, which symbolizes one's
grief. Likewise, the mourners are not to go to work and are to
refrain from any enjoyable activities. Grief is further expressed in Jewish tradition by the family sitting on low stools
or removing cushions from their furniture.

Due to the intensity of "sitting shiva," it is considered a
mitzvah (good deed) to provide the first meal for the family at

home. This practice may extend for the entire week. It is common for condolences from visitors to be received at this time. Many times, comforters give a donation to the synagogue or other charity as a memorial to the deceased.

The seven day *shiva* period telescopes into the next time frame for mourning, called *shloshim* ("thirty"). This thirty-day period could be classified as a time of semi-mourning. The intensity of *shiva* is completed; hence, make-up, shaving and the regular work schedule can be restarted. However, the grieving continues in that there is no participation in music, parties or weddings.

The final period of mourning, *avelut*, starts after the *shloshim* and extends for a full year, by the Hebrew calendar, from the date of death. One's daily life continues to normalize, yet with the constant reminder of the loss of the loved one. *Kaddish* is recited daily, preferably in the synagogue, for the first eleven months. This is ceased before completion of the twelve months, because of the belief by the talmudic rabbis that the final fate of the wicked is determined over the full year. Consequently, it would be a statement of presumption and judgment if the prayers continued through the complete year (Klein, A *Guide to Jewish Religious Practice*, p. 293). On this one-year anniversary of the death (called the *yahrzeit*), the unveiling or stone setting commonly takes place. Also, a special *yahrzeit* candle is lit every year on this anniversary date in remembrance of the deceased. This custom, based on Proverbs 20:27, illustrates the truth that

"the lamp of the LORD searches the spirit of a man." Another familiar custom is that of leaving a small stone on the grave marker after a visit to show that the person is not forgotten. These are all special ways to honor the life and memory of the loved one.

While some people may not understand or appreciate some of these customs, there are many benefits to the Jewish approach to death. Clearly, respect and honor are of the utmost importance in regard to the deceased. There are also great benefits found for the mourners in many of these customs. Too often, modern analytical society does not properly cope with death. Yet, the structure of the *shiva* and other mourning periods encourage openness and healing at the time of grief. In the words of Solomon, there is "a time to weep and a time to laugh, a time to mourn and a time to dance" (Ecclesiastes 3:4). Many psychologists and counselors are finding new truth in the ancient ways of Torah and the Jewish traditions. God's appointed customs have much to teach, as one looks beyond the surface to see the God who desires to be each person's personal comforter.

RELEVANCE TO THE NEW TESTAMENT

Many of the customs associated with the Jewish way of death and mourning illustrate the truths of the Hebrew Scriptures. The reality of death and the healthy ways of mourning are both addressed through the ancient traditions that are practiced to this day. What is not so well known is that many of these same customs are a part of the New Testament culture. After all, the earliest disciples of Yeshua not only lived a Jewish lifestyle but died as observant Jews as well. It is quite enlightening to see many of the New Testament incidents set against the cultural backdrop of the first-century Jewish community.

Of the several accounts that touched on the issues of death in the New Testament, the most dramatic was centered on the death and resurrection of Yeshua. For believers, this part of New Testament history is most central to their faith. As one develops an understanding of the customs surrounding Yeshua's death, the depths of its meaning will begin to be appreciated even more.

After the religious and civil trials of Yeshua found him guilty, the Romans had him executed in their conventional manner of crucifixion. It was an agonizing death, yet one that would fulfill prophecy and purchase redemption for those who believe in him (see Isaiah 53; Daniel 9). His death presented the problem of what to do with the body of this controversial rabbi/Messiah. Would one of the disciples step forward to claim the body at risk of further persecution and trouble? Would they just let the Romans bury him like a common criminal? It must have been a surprise to everyone when *Yosef* of *Ramatayim* ("Joseph of Arimathea") stepped forward to assist with the burial.

> Since it was Preparation Day (that is, the day before a Shabbat), as evening approached, Yosef of Ramatayim, a prominent member of the Sanhedrin who himself was also looking forward to the Kingdom of God, went boldly to Pilate and asked for Yeshua's body. Pilate was surprised to hear that he was already dead, so he summoned the officer and asked him if he had been dead awhile. After he had gotten confirmation from the officer that Yeshua was dead, he granted Yosef the corpse (Mark 15:42–45).

This striking description teaches several things that are often misunderstood about the death of Yeshua. Too often it is assumed that "the Jews" (meaning every single Jew) rejected Yeshua. However, a careful reading of the Gospels dictates something quite different. Was it not during this same week that a great multitude of Jewish people welcomed Yeshua to Jerusalem with the messianic blessing, *Barukh habah b'shem Adonai* ("Blessed is he who comes in the name of Adonai"; see Mark 11:8–9). Was it not Jewish people who wept and grieved as Yeshua was led to Golgotha (see Luke 23:27)? Could all of these supporters have suddenly changed their minds and joined in the condemnation of the Son of David?

The simple answer is this: there were clearly those who rejected the Messiahship of Yeshua; yet, there was a strong minority who maintained their trust in him. This minority may have been confused regarding those bleak events that transpired in Jerusalem, but they were the remnant that would have such an impact in that same city after the resurrection. There is no doubt that Yeshua and his Messianic followers caused quite a controversy. However, it is because of this controversy that one knows that it was a split decision. There were many Jewish people on each side of the controversy.

There were even those on the seventy-member *Sanhedrin* who actually believed that Yeshua was the Messiah. Obviously *Yosef*, and his rabbinic colleague Nicodemus (*Nakdimon*), did not vote for the conviction of Yeshua. The chances are that they were not even part of the quorum present when the evening proceedings took place (see John 19:38–39). Nonetheless, the sentiments of the majority won out and Yeshua was executed on the basis of the charge of blasphemy.

Although somewhat surprising that *Yosef* claimed the body of Yeshua, what followed was quite consistent with the Jewish burial customs of that day.

> Yosef purchased a linen sheet; and after taking Yeshua down, he wrapped him in the linen sheet, laid him in a tomb which had been cut out of the rock, and rolled a stone against the entrance to the tomb. Miryam of Magdala and Miryam the mother of Yosi saw where he had been laid (Mark 15:46–47).

As was common, *Yosef* followed the custom of *takhrikhim* by providing the proper burial garment. It seems that he and *Nakdimon* also performed the *mitzvah* of beginning to prepare the body for burial, the duty of the *Chevra Kaddisha* (see John 19:38–39). However, there were some logistical problems. A *shabbat* was quickly approaching and there was not sufficient time to complete the preparation before the holy day began. So *Yosef* and those with him hurriedly placed the body of Yeshua in a tomb owned by *Yosef* and sealed it up until the close of the *shabbat*. Consistent with Jewish custom, the full burial would be completed at the soonest opportunity.

What happened next changed the course of Jewish and world history! Mark's account is as follows:

When Shabbat was over, Miryam of Magdala, Miryam the mother of Ya'akov, and Shlomit [Salome] bought spices in order to go and anoint Yeshua. Very early on Sunday, just after sunrise, they went to the tomb. They were asking each other, "Who will roll away the stone from the entrance to the tomb for us?" Then they looked up and saw that the stone, even though it was huge, had been rolled back already. On entering the tomb, they saw a young man dressed in a white robe sitting on the right; and they were dumbfounded. But he said, "Don't be so surprised! You're looking for Yeshua from Natzeret, who was executed on the stake. He is not here, he has risen! Look at the place where they laid him" (Mark 16:1–6).

In Jewish tradition the body of the deceased is treated with utmost respect. The female disciples came after the *shabbat* to complete the cleansing and preparation that the *Chevra Kaddisha* (*Yosef*, *Nakdimon* and others) started. It is of course forbidden to embalm or alter the body in any way. However, to anoint the shrouded body with perfumes and spices, in preparation for a completed burial, was quite appropriate.

Everything changed on that early morning in Jerusalem. The body was gone. The women and other disciples never wondered if somehow the body was stolen, because the *takhrikhim* garments were mysteriously still in place (see John 20:5–8). What else could they do but believe the words of the angelic messenger: "He's not here, he is risen!" They had witnessed the ultimate proof that Yeshua of Natzeret is the Messiah; God had raised him from the dead. Yeshua actually appeared in his glorified body to hundreds of his Jewish followers, thereby validating his resurrection (see 1 Corinthians 15:1–8).

It is interesting to see how the Jewish burial customs are followed in the New Testament. However, what is even more important is to examine the reason for the death, burial and resurrection of Yeshua. He paid for the sins of the world by his vicarious death. Likewise, he was buried in a rich man's tomb in fulfillment of the Scriptures (see Isaiah 53). Yet, it is the

Messiah's victory over death, through the resurrection, that had the most dramatic impact on this world and the world to come. Death, both physical and spiritual, has been defeated. As Saul of Tarsus said:

> Look, I will tell you a secret—not all of us will die! But we will all be changed! It will take but a moment, the blink of an eye, at the final shofar. For the shofar will sound, and the dead will be raised to live forever, and we too will be changed. For this material which can decay must be clothed with imperishability, this which is mortal must be clothed with immortality. When what decays puts on imperishability and what is mortal puts on immortality, then this passage in the Tanakh will be fulfilled:
>
> > "Death is swallowed up in victory.
> > Death, where is your victory?
> > Death, where is your sting?"
> > The sting of death is sin; and sin draws its power from the Torah; but thanks be to God, who gives us the victory through our Lord Yeshua the Messiah (1 Corinthians 15:51–57)!

This is the "Good News." As one considers the Jewish ways of death and mourning, one needs to ask if he or she can be sure of their place in the *olam habah* ("the world to come"). Each person, Jew and Gentile, needs to ask if he or she has embraced Yeshua, the living redeemer, who has opened the way of forgiveness as God's appointed Messiah.

PRACTICAL GUIDE FOR A MESSIANIC FUNERAL

As with all of the biblical/Jewish customs, there is freedom to make any personal adjustments in the structure. Most importantly, the service should be personalized to reflect the family's hope of the coming Messiah. The following is a suggested order of service.

INTRODUCTORY MUSIC

OPENING SCRIPTURE READINGS
Passages from the Psalms (e.g., Psalm 46, 116, 121, etc.)—It is good to give a proper introduction and context to this special service, explaining what it means to a believer in Yeshua. Some additional suggested Scriptures might include any of the following: Job 19, John 11, 1 Corinthians 15, 1 Thessalonians 4, etc.

MESSIANIC LEADER'S MESSAGE

EULOGY OR TESTIMONIES FROM FAMILY OR FRIENDS

SPECIAL MUSIC

KADDISH Explained and Recited (refer to Scherman, *The Rabbinical Council of America Edition of The Artscroll Siddur*—see the bibliography—or any other traditional *siddur*)

CLOSING PRAYER BY MESSIANIC LEADER
A closing prayer may center on hope for believers and comfort for the mourners.

It is a blessing to have the assurance that personal faith in the Messiah Yeshua will provide the blessings of the resurrection in his coming kingdom. However, understanding the biblical/Jewish ways of dealing with death and mourning are useful in this life.

Part 2

Biblical
Lifestyle

6

M'zuzah

The Doorpost

THE HISTORICAL BACKGROUND

Hear, O Israel: The Lord our God, the Lord is one. Love the Lord your God with all your heart and with all your soul and with all your strength. These command- ments that I give you today are to be upon your hearts. Impress them on your children. Talk about them when you sit at home and when you walk along the road, when you lie down and when you get up. Tie them as symbols on your hands and bind them on your fore- heads. Write them on the doorframes of your houses and on your gates (Deuteronomy 6:4–9).

The *m'zuzah* is a small box that is attached to the doors of people's homes. It has a powerful message. To this day, it is a sign of a household that honors God and is dedicated to his service. Where did this distinctive custom arise from?

The Hebrew word *m'zuzah* is the word for the doorjamb or frame. In biblical times, the doorpost of a house represented the family and its values. Due to its visibility, the doorpost was a place to show one's identity. Thus, it is not surprising that God commanded the blood of the first Passover lamb to be applied to the *m'zuzah* ("doorpost") of each Israelite household (see Exodus 12:21–22). The Torah also commanded a slave, who voluntarily wanted to stay with his master, to have his ear pierced at the *m'zuzah* (see Exodus 21:6). Significantly, God required those people who fear his name to publicly display his commandments on the *m'zuzah* of their houses (see Deuteronomy 6:9).

The manner in which this custom was actually observed took various forms in Jewish history. It could have been literally fulfilled by inscribing the doorpost itself with the Word of God. Some historians speculate that this would have been a direct response to the common pagan custom of placing magical charms or amulets on their doors to ward off evil spirits. Unfortunately, many Jews throughout history *have* mistakenly attributed magical powers to the presence of the *m'zuzah* on the door. This practice was strongly denounced by rabbinic authorities, including the great commentator Maimonides.

> Those fools not only fail to fulfill the mitzvah itself, but they have taken a great mitzvah, which involves the Oneness of God and the reminder to love Him and worship Him, and treat it as though it were an amulet designed to benefit them personally . . . (Birnbaum, *Mishneh Torah*, Mezuzah 5:4).

Contrary to such superstition, the *m'zuzah* should be a reminder that the God of Israel protects, not by magic, but by the power of his word.

Over time, the custom evolved that a small container would be attached to the doorpost. This box was called a *m'zuzah* and took various functional shapes and artistic designs. To be more accurate, the *m'zuzah* is the parchment containing the Hebrew Scriptures; the box is merely the ceremonial container. However, the whole container, including the parchment, is usually called the *m'zuzah*.

In first-century Israel, the *m'zuzah* was a common custom. The Jewish historian, Josephus, in describing the first-century community in Israel, wrote:

> They are also to inscribe the principal blessing they have received from God upon their doors, and show the same remembrance of them upon their arms . . . (Whiston, *Josephus' Complete Works*, Antiquities 4:8:13).

The recent archaeological digs at Qumran have not only revealed a vast collection of manuscripts, but also various kinds of *m'zuzot* (plural of *m'zuzah*). As Rabbinic Judaism developed after the destruction of the Temple (70 C.E.), the rabbis prescribed detailed laws on how the custom of *m'zuzah* should be followed. These laws included how the parchment was to be written, which verses of Torah should be included, and how the *m'zuzah* should be attached. However, the diversity of the Jewish community in the dispersion led to the development of many variations and local customs. Nevertheless, after thousands of years of history, the modern usage of this custom has stayed remarkably consistent. The *m'zuzah* remains a constant reminder to follow the God of Israel.

TRADITIONAL JEWISH OBSERVANCE

The practice of affixing a *m'zuzah* continues to be quite popular. The appearance of the outer case may range from traditional Jewish themes to a child's toy car. Often the container will have the Hebrew letter *shin* on the outside, the first letter of an important attribute of God, *Shaddai* ("Almighty"). In addition, the three Hebrew letters that form the word *Shaddai*, Sh–D–Y, are an acronym that stands for *Shomeyr daltot Yisraeyl* ("Watchman of the doors of Israel").

The most important part of the ceremonial item is the parchment inside the container. This is actually the most costly part of the *m'zuzah*, since a scribe has hand written two biblical passages (Deuteronomy 6:4–9 and Deuteronomy 11:13–21) on a "kosher" parchment (i.e., animal skin). This tiny scroll is then rolled up with the Scripture facing in; however, the word for God's name, *Shaddai*, appears on the outside of the rolled parchment.

The Orthodox rabbis determined that *m'zuzot* should be placed on every doorframe of the permanent dwelling places. This includes exterior doorways to homes and all interior doorways. It even includes courtyards or fenced-in areas, since the Bible says it should be written "upon your gates." Although it is not legally required, it is common to see a *m'zuzah* on the doors of public buildings in Israel, or in synagogues as well. The only exception is for rooms that are not considered dignified, such as bathrooms or bathhouses (Donin, *To Be a Jew*, p. 153).

The *m'zuzah* is normally affixed to a new home or apartment as soon as possible, although the rabbis allow thirty days to fulfill this commandment. Anyone older than *Bar Mitzvah* age, male or female, is permitted to attach the *m'zuzah*. Before nailing or gluing the *m'zuzah* to the doorway, the following blessing is recited:

Barukh atah Adonai, eloheynu melekh ha'olam, asher kidshanu b'mitzvotav v'tzivanu likboa m'zuzah.

Blessed art Thou, O Lord our God, King of the universe, who has sanctified us by His commandments and commanded us to affix a m'zuzah.

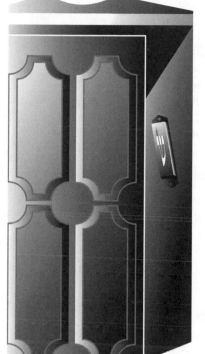

The exact positioning of the *m'zuzah* on the doorway can vary depending on the customs of a particular Jewish community. It is a universal practice to place the container on the right side of the doorway as one enters a room, in the upper third portion. Sephardic Jews (those from Spain or Mediterranean lands) often affix the *m'zuzah* in a straight vertical position. The Ashkenazi Jews (those whose roots are from eastern Europe) practice the tradition of slanting the top of the *m'zuzah* towards the room. These varying customs reflect a rabbinic debate in the Middle Ages. The esteemed Rashi (Rabbi *Shlomo ben Yitzkhak*) stated that the *m'zuzah* should be attached vertically; yet, his grandson, *Rabbeynu Tam*, believed it should be in a horizontal position. In a classic rabbinic compromise, it was decided that the *m'zuzah* should be slanted to reflect both views (Birnbaum, A *Book of Jewish Concepts*, p. 349).

Out of respect for this important custom, it is common to see people touch the *m'zuzah* as they pass through the doorway. Specifically, one is to kiss the fingers and touch the word *Shaddai* to show one's love for God. A tangential custom that has become popular among contemporary Jews is to wear jewelry in the shape of a *m'zuzah*. Although a necklace is different from the doorway *m'zuzah*, it is considered a beautiful way to identify with one's Jewishness and to remember the commandments.

The *m'zuzah* is an important custom that God has appointed to help his people remember him and his ways.

Relevance To The New Testament

Although there is no specific reference in the New Testament to the custom of affixing a *m'zuzah*, there are a number of interesting principles that would apply to it. For example, Yeshua affirmed the truth contained in the *m'zuzah*. When Yeshua was asked by a rabbi which commandment he considered to be the most important, he responded with the passage found in the *m'zuzah*:

Sh'ma Israel, Adonai Eloheynu, Adonai echad

Hear, O Israel, the Lord our God, the Lord is one (Mark 12:29; cf., Deuteronomy 6:4–5).

The words of Yeshua become more meaningful in light of the significance of doorways and gates in Jewish culture. As he explained to his disciples:

. . . "Yes, indeed! I tell you that I am the gate for the sheep. All those who have come before me have been thieves and robbers, but the sheep didn't listen to them. I am the gate; if someone enters through me, he will be safe and will go in and out and find pasture. The thief comes only in order to steal, kill and destroy; I have come so that they may have life, life in its fullest measure" (John 10:7–10).

The door or gate was vital. It was the place of entry to find protection. Likewise, it was the place through which to enter to receive the provision of the shepherd or landowner. As an entrance into Jewish property, the door and gate would have been marked as dedicated to God by the custom of the *m'zuzah* (see Deuteronomy 6:9).

Yeshua used the symbolism associated with the *m'zuzah* to point out that he was the entrance to the Father. While many people might believe that faith in Yeshua leads to restrictions, Yeshua actually asserted that those who follow his ways will find the fullest measure of life. What could be more fulfilling than walking in the perfect will of the Father, as taught by the Jewish Messiah? The symbolism of the *m'zuzah* (i.e., the blessings of walking in God's commandments) is perfectly understood in light of Yeshua being the gate that leads to spiritual life.

For those who are already believers in the Messiah, there is a further lesson to be gleaned from the custom of the *m'zuzah*. The small container marks a house that is dedicated to following God. Likewise, believers in Yeshua are called a spiritual house that is dedicated to the glory of God. Saul alluded to this in his letter to the Gentile believers in Ephesus when he said:

> So then, you are no longer foreigners and strangers. On the contrary, you are fellow-citizens with God's people [i.e., the Jewish remnant] and members of God's family. You have built on the foundation of the emissaries and the prophets, with the cornerstone being Yeshua the Messiah himself. In union with him the whole building is held together, and it is growing into a holy temple in union with the Lord. Yes, in union with him, you yourselves are being built together into a spiritual dwelling-place for God (Ephesians 2:19–22)!

The message of the *m'zuzah* is simple yet powerful. Is the home dedicated to the glory and service of God? More importantly, have the people opened the door of their hearts to allow the Messiah to dwell with them daily?

> Here, I'm standing at the door, knocking. If someone hears my voice and opens the door, I will come in to him an eat with him, and he will eat with me (Revelation 3:20).

PRACTICAL GUIDE FOR AFFIXING A M'ZUZAH

An understanding of the significance of the *m'zuzah* enables Messianic believers to follow this custom with joy.

Even in the secular world, it is not uncommon for people to have a "house-warming party" to celebrate their new home. It is much more meaningful for believers in Yeshua, Jewish or non-Jewish, to incorporate a house dedication ceremony that acknowledges God. The public display of *m'zuzot* would be not only a reminder to the owners of their own covenant with God, but it would serve as a testimony to visitors of the owners' personal faith and connection with the Jewish people.

As mentioned previously, in keeping with ancient tradition, the *m'zuzah* is usually placed on a new dwelling within the first thirty days of occupying it. A *m'zuzah* is usually placed on every doorway of the house, except for the bathrooms. However, the minimum requirement for observant Jews is a *m'zuzah* on the front door.

Prior to affixing the container, the following blessing is recited:

Barukh atah Adonai, eloheynu melekh ha'olam, asher kidshanu b'mitzvotav v'tzivanu likboa m'zuzah.

Blessed art Thou, O Lord our God, King of the universe, who has sanctified us by his commandments and commanded us to affix a m'zuzah.

The *m'zuzah* is nailed or glued to the right side of the doorpost, with the top of the container slanted towards the room. In addition to the traditional blessings and verses, it is appropriate to share some New Testament Scriptures relevant to the meaning of the *m'zuzah* and have a time of personal prayer.

May God's appointed custom of the *m'zuzah* be a blessing to all. May believers in Yeshua affirm in a new way: "But as for me and my household, we will serve the LORD" (Joshua 24:15).

7

Kashrut

Dietary Laws

THE HISTORICAL BACKGROUND

The LORD said to Moses and Aaron, "Say to the Israelites: 'Of all the animals that live on land, these are the ones you may eat. You may eat any animal that has a split hoof completely divided and that chews the cud. There are some that only chew the cud or only have a split hoof, but you must not eat them.' . . . 'Of all the creatures living in the water of the seas and the streams, you may eat any that have fins and scales. But all creatures in the seas or streams that do not have fins and scales—whether among all the swarming things or among all the other living creatures in the water—you are to detest.' . . . 'These are the regulations concerning animals, birds, every living thing that moves in the water and every creature that moves about on the ground. You must distinguish between the unclean and the clean, between living creatures that may be eaten and those that may not be eaten'" (Leviticus 11:1–4, 9–10, 46–47).

One of the more important customs given by God to the Jewish people is that of *kashrut* (noun form of "kosher," the dietary laws). If anything has distinguished Israel over the generations, it is the fact that they had a special diet to follow. The reasons for these unusual customs can be better understood by thinking of God's overall plan for his covenant people. They are his nation set-apart to accomplish his will. The Jewish people have always had the mandate to teach the nations about the uniqueness of the God of Abraham, Isaac and Jacob.

On the one hand, there are many physical and health benefits to the dietary laws, especially in the ancient Middle East. However, it should not be overlooked that there are many vital spiritual lessons to be learned from the tradition of *kashrut*. The religious nature of diet and foods have always been emphasized in Judaism, as is seen in the following quote:

> Various aspects of the meal—all of which go to sanctify it—are connected to this thought of the table being an altar. The meal is made holy by blessings before and after, through Torah and song, through charity and through meditation. On the higher levels of spiritual attainment, the motive in eating should not be to satisfy our personal need or pleasure, but should be connected to God and be a service of God. Eating is to be a devotional act (Buxbaum, *Jewish Spiritual Practices*, p. 226).

An understanding of *kashrut* can be gained by taking a deeper look at Leviticus 11, the central passage on *kashrut*. Long after the redemption of the children of Israel from Egypt, God spoke in some detail on how his covenant people should live. However, it is noteworthy that *kashrut* has nothing to do with one's salvation experience. In context, these commandments were given to those who already knew God as their Father. The Leviticus 11 passage describes events that took place long after the "salvation" experience depicted in Exodus 14. As with all the customs appointed by God, they were given to help believers remember and appreciate what God has done for them by his grace.

As believers in Yeshua the Messiah, it is crucial to study the truths of the Torah through the lens of the full revelation of the New Testament. Messiah has come and believers should expect that he would explain the spiritual meaning of the Jewish customs, including *kashrut*. In many ways, Messianic Jews and like-minded Gentiles are returning to a true Torah understanding of the dietary laws.

Chapter 11 of Leviticus is the most detailed account of the principles for *kashrut*. It details the laws concerning mammals in the first eight verses. The clean animals that are permissible for food are described as *tahor* (a Hebrew synonym for "kosher"). The qualifications for these mammals are that they must both chew the cud and have a split hoof (e.g., the cow and sheep). However, there are also mammals that are classified as *tamey* ("unclean"). In the vernacular of the Jewish people, it is normal to refer to any unkosher food as *tareyf*.

There are many animals that neither chew the cud nor have a split hoof that are clearly disqualified and are not listed in the Bible. It is interesting to note the animals mentioned that meet one of the two requirements. For example, the camel chews the cud but does not have a split hoof. Most people automatically regard the pig as the ultimate in non-kosher animals, yet it is specifically listed in Leviticus 11 because it actually matches one of the requirements—it has a split hoof.

Why was it necessary to have a split hoof? All the animals listed that meet this requirement are herbivores, that is, vegetation eaters. Being vegetarian helped Israel avoid some unhealthy parasites that often develop in meat eaters. The pig is an omnivore, meaning that it is not picky at all in what it eats, either vegetation or meat.

Why was it necessary to chew the cud? These animals are known to have much more effective digestive systems (i.e., two, or even three stomachs) that serve as a filter against potentially harmful elements in the food. Those mammals that do not chew the cud swallow whatever they eat, which is quickly transferred into their bloodstream. One can begin to appreciate the wisdom of the Torah in these details.

Assuming that a mammal is *tahor* ("kosher"), there is yet another disqualifying factor that may apply. If the animal died a violent death that might have damaged its body or organs, it was *t'reyfah* (see Exodus 22:31). This Hebrew term literally means "torn" and graphically describes an animal that is killed by wild beasts. This commandment seems to be tied to the fact that the Scriptures place a high value on blood. Due to this respect for the blood, the animal also had to be slaughtered in the proper manner. For the same reasons, the Torah also excludes eating any animal, even kosher ones, that died a natural death (see Leviticus 11:39–40). This type of animal is called a *n'veylah* ("carcass") and is "off-limits" because it has not been slaughtered; hence, it retains its blood.

In Leviticus, there are set definitions for determining whether a fish is kosher or not (see Leviticus 11:9–12). The fish must have both fins and scales. These characteristics include a great deal of fish, but exclude a number of notable species. The shark and catfish fit the non-kosher description. They have no scales. Those without fins refer to any kind of shellfish, including lobster and shrimp.

Why does it matter if the fish have fins or scales? Those fish without fins or scales are usually the scavengers of the oceans. Therefore, these species contain high levels of toxins (e.g., mercury) and a high cholesterol. They are certainly part of God's creation. Such scavengers were meant to be the "garbage disposals" of their world. This is a needed function; however, they are not meant to be eaten as food by God's covenant people.

Similar ideas can be seen in the laws concerning kosher and unkosher fowl (see Leviticus 11:13–19). While no general description is mentioned as to what the qualifications are for kosher and *tareyf*, the Bible gives a short list of birds that were considered *tareyf*. The eagle, vulture and the owl are examples of such birds that are not to be eaten. What is the connection?

As with the *tareyf* category of fish, these creatures are all birds of prey or scavengers. It is noteworthy that many of these birds have been endangered in recent years (notably the California condor) because of the high toxicity that they take in through their diet. Since they are scavengers, they are on the bottom of the food chain. Therefore, they ingest the greatest concentration of substances causing the problems affecting the animal kingdom at large, for example, chemicals and pollution. These birds serve an important function in helping to clean up the environment, but they are not meant to be food.

One final category highlighted in the Torah is that of insects and creatures that move on the ground (see Leviticus 11:20–23, 42–43). This includes any snake or lizard as well as such dietary treats as *escargot* ("snails") or chocolate covered ants. These insects and creatures that move on the ground were not intended to be food.

Why did God tell his people Israel to follow such a specialized diet? The reasons seem to be two-fold. The initial supposition is that there are inherent health benefits to *kashrut*. It is often pointed out that these laws have provided important health protection, especially in the ancient Middle East. Before the days of refrigeration, these laws protected Israel from such health problems as trichinosis, commonly found in pork.

Although this might be reason enough to appreciate the principles of *kashrut*, there seems to be a much more important reason why God gave these laws to the Jewish people. Simple health considerations cannot explain all the details of *kashrut*; a goat or a barnyard chicken can live a dirtier existence than a camel or even a pig. The more important reason for *kashrut* is summarized by Rabbi Donin:

> In fact, the terms used in Hebrew to designate the clean and unclean animals are tahor and tamai. These are terms that are never used to describe physical

cleanliness or uncleanliness, but rather a spiritual or moral state of being. The term tamai is used only in relation to moral and religious deficiencies that contaminate the soul and character of man, particularly incest and idol worship, and to characterize the absence of ritual purity. It is often also translated as defilement. The creatures designated as tamai were not only forbidden as food, but also for sacrificial purposes. The English words clean and unclean are therefore to be understood as purity and defilement in a spiritual-ritual sense (Donin, To Be a Jew, p. 99).

This points to the summary statement found in Leviticus pertaining to the ultimate purpose of all the dietary laws:

I am the LORD who brought you up out of Egypt to be your God; therefore be holy, because I am holy (Leviticus 11:45).

The spiritual symbolism is much more important than the health benefits found in kashrut. Israel was called to be a distinct people, holy or set-apart for God's purposes. There was no better way to keep his people distinct from the pagan nations than to give them a separate diet. Every meal reminded the observant Jew that his calling was different from the world. Since God is set-apart and unique, so too his children should be set-apart and unique. Understood this way, one can appreciate the details of kashrut as a custom appointed by God to help his children remember who they are and how they are to live.

TRADITIONAL JEWISH OBSERVANCE

The emphasis that the Torah places upon the dietary laws has caused the Jewish community to continue these practices from generation to generation. However, the rabbis added many finer points to the understanding of kashrut.

The rabbis grappled with the laws concerning exactly *how* a kosher animal was to be slaughtered. Because the *n'veylah* ("carcass") and *t'reyfah* animals were not to be eaten, it was understood that even kosher animals must be slaughtered in a ritual manner. The only exceptions to this were fish that were already considered acceptable based on Numbers 11:22 ("flocks and herds were slaughtered . . . [but] fish in the sea were caught"). The slaughtering procedure is called *sh'khitah*, the noun form of the word in Deuteronomy 12:21, "you may *slaughter* animals . . ." Although the Bible gives no additional details on how this slaughter of animals is to occur, the rabbis developed an elaborate system for *sh'khitah*. This ritual way of slaughter is carried out by the kosher butcher known as a *shokhet*, who must be a pious Jew, respected in the community. He performs his duties as a religious obligation while saying the appropriate Hebrew blessings.

There are a number of aspects to rabbinic *sh'khitah*. First, it should be noted that this type of ritual slaughter is considered the least painful to the animal. The procedure is simple; a flawless knife is used by the *shokhet* to cut the throat of the animal. This technique is used to sever the major nerves, which immediately renders the animal unconscious. This is also the best way to remove the blood from the animal, since it severs major arteries and veins. This fulfills the biblical prohibition against eating blood by not letting it congeal within the meat.

While there is considerable debate today about animal rights and cruelty to animals, it has been found that the *sh'khitah* method of slaughter is perhaps the most humane. Many modern methods of stunning the animals before slaughter actually inflict injuries on the animals that would render them non-kosher. Many doctors and scientists have agreed that because the *sh'khitah* method renders the animal instantly insensitive, the Jewish way of ritual slaughter is eminently humane (Donin, *To Be a Jew*, p. 107).

Even with the strict guidelines of *sh'khitah*, there are additional ways in which meat is to be koshered before eating. To guarantee that no more than the minimum amount of blood is left in the meat, Jewish tradition specifies that one of two methods be followed. The first method involves soaking and salting the meat. This takes place by thoroughly washing the meat and immersing it in water to soak for one-half hour. At that point, the meat is removed from the water and completely covered with coarse, "koshering salt" for a period of one hour. Then the meat is once again rinsed, this time to remove all traces of salt and any blood drawn out by the salt. Many times the *shokhet* will kosher the meat in this manner before it is sold to the customer. If not, it is the duty of the cook to prepare the meat in this way. The meat is then ready to be cooked in whatever manner desired. It is assumed that the blood has been removed.

The other method of removing the excess blood is simply to broil the meat on a grill (not a pan) so that the blood may drip off away from the meat. This method is normally used only when soaking and salting are not practical (e.g., when cooking chicken livers).

It should be noted that kosher frozen meats are also available in many grocery stores. These have been koshered in the described manner before being packaged and sold. They will bear a seal of *kashrut* (e.g., U or k) from one of the Orthodox rabbinic boards, indicating that they are kosher.

Another rabbinic interpretation of *kashrut* is the separation of milk and meat products. This is derived from the rather oblique reference in the Torah, "Do not cook a young goat in its mother's milk" (Exodus 23:19). The ancient authorities said that in order to ensure that this commandment is not broken, one should abstain from eating milk and meat together at the same meal. Interestingly, Maimonides understood this to be a prohibition against following a grotesque Canaanite religious practice. Thus, this law is another example of God telling Israel not to follow the ways of the pagans around them.

The implications of this tradition are immense. A traditional Jew must take care not only to have kosher meat but also not to mix the meat with any milk product. Thus, there is no such thing as a kosher cheeseburger. In addition, this means that separate sets of dishes and silverware must be used to ensure that there is no contact between the milk and meat. In Yiddish, this is designated as *milchig* (dairy) and *fleishig* (meat) dishes and silverware. In addition, there is a need for separate pots and containers for milk and meat products. There is a way to kosher the dishes and containers (by boiling or scorching with a flame), but since it is so labor intensive, the easier option is to have a separate set of utensils. There is an entire tractate of the Talmud devoted to what constitutes a kosher or non-kosher container (*Babylonian Talmud*, Kelim).

There are also some foods that are considered neutral (e.g., vegetables, chocolate, soft drinks, etc.) and these are called *parve*. They may be served with either milk or meat. In our modern society, there are new options for kosher cooking that include margarine and non-dairy creamers. In practical terms, an observant Jew must take great care to not eat milk and meat together, but wait a set period of time before eating from another category of food. While the Talmud does not specifically define the length of time, a common practice is to wait at least six hours, or until the next meal, after eating *fleishig*, before eating *milchig*. Since milk is more easily digested than meat, it is acceptable to eat *fleishig* shortly after a *milchig* meal. In addition, *milchig* and *fleishig* must be stored separately in a refrigerator, and the dishes must be washed separately. Some people, for convenience, even use two dishwashers to guarantee *kashrut*.

Another important custom associated with *kashrut* is the exclusion of the sciatic nerve, which runs through the hind quarter of an animal. This is actually based on the biblical command from the story of Jacob wrestling with the Angel of the LORD (see Genesis 32:32). Although some remove the sciatic nerve in the koshering process, it is often considered too labor intensive to make a profit. More often, the hind quarter is simply not used in kosher cooking.

Additionally, the Bible prohibits the eating of certain kinds of fats, usually that surrounding the vital organs. This is in contradistinction to the fat around the muscles, and the skin, which are permissible.

This brief overview illustrates how daunting the kosher lifestyle can be. The rules are many. There have been people who have lost perspective of the intent of *kashrut* and fell into legalism. However, when properly understood, one will gain a greater appreciation for the spiritual truths of the Torah. All that is done should be a reminder of the covenant with God. The Jewish people are a distinct, holy, set-apart people. Even the very diet of the Jews is a constant reminder of their calling to be a "kosher" people in this world.

RELEVANCE TO THE NEW TESTAMENT

It will be a surprise to some that *kashrut* has any relevance at all to the New Testament. So often it is brushed off as merely one of those archaic customs of the Law. However, *kashrut* is raised as an important topic of discussion several times in the New Testament. It was a very important issue as Jews began to believe in Yeshua. An even bigger question arose when Gentiles started believing in Yeshua. Were they to live a kosher lifestyle since they accepted the Jewish Messiah? In a discourse to the Jewish crowds, Yeshua said:

> ... "Listen to me, all of you, and understand this! There is nothing outside a person which, by going into him, can make him unclean. Rather, it is the things that come out of a person which make a person unclean!" When he had left the people and entered the house, his talmidim asked him about the parable. He replied to them, "So you too are without understanding? Don't you see that nothing going into a person from outside can make him unclean? For it doesn't go into his heart but into his stomach, and it passes out into the latrine." (Thus he declared all foods ritually clean.) "It is what comes out of a person," he went on, "that makes him unclean. For from within, out of a person's heart, come forth wicked thoughts, sexual immorality,

theft, murder, adultery, greed, malice, deceit, inde-
cency, envy, slander, arrogance, foolishness. All these
wicked things come from within, and they make a
person unclean" (Mark 7:14–23).

These must have been shocking words to those Jewish
disciples. They sound no less shocking to Jewish ears today.
It is often presumed by both Christian and Jewish theologians
that these words of Yeshua negate all of *kashrut*. However, this
interpretation becomes difficult when compared with other
statements by Yeshua, where he clearly upholds every letter
of the Torah (see Matthew 5:17). It is beyond dispute that the
Messiah was teaching that the higher principle of the dietary
laws was always to be spiritual. God is always looking at the
heart before the diet.

However, a closer look at the context of Mark 7 reveals
that Yeshua was not primarily addressing the aspect of foods,
but was referring to ritual washings. It is clearly stated that
this whole discussion was started by rabbis who were condemning Yeshua's disciples for not properly *washing* their
hands or *koshering* their dishes (see Mark 7:1–4). This is further
confirmed by that fact that part of Messiah's answer to the
rabbis was that it is not what is outside (i.e., unclean hands
or vessels) that is the issue.

The question was *not* one of non-kosher foods. Presumably, the food under discussion was considered biblically
kosher. The main question was whether or not this kosher
food would be rendered as *tareyf* because the disciples did not
follow the rabbinic practices. Contrary to popular belief,
Yeshua was not pronouncing the arrival of "kosher bacon,"
but was simply affirming the priority of the Scriptures over the
authority of the rabbis. Another key to this passage is in the
Jewish definition of the word "foods" (verse 19). In light of the
Jewish understanding of what was considered food and of
what was not food, one can see that Yeshua was not annulling
the biblical precepts of the dietary laws. From the Jewish
perspective, the pig, dog and snail, for example, were *not*
considered "foods" for consumption. Clearly, there is a context to these statements that must not be ignored. In this

passage, Yeshua affirmed that a kosher steak did not become unclean just because all the rabbinic guidelines were not followed (Juster, *Jewish Roots*, p. 126).

Many believers credit Saul of Tarsus with changing the dietary laws. Romans 14 deals with the *kashrut* issue. Saul's conclusions led him to the important guideline of freedom based on one's personal convictions.

However, a closer look at this chapter shows that the issue was not one of permitting a Jew to eat non-kosher food; the issue was one of eating meat versus being a *vegetarian*. In his letter to the young Jewish believer, Timothy, Saul wrote concerning his convictions about personal diet:

> They [false teachers] forbid marriage and require abstinence from foods which God created to be eaten with thanksgiving by those who have come to trust and to know the truth. For everything created by God is good, and nothing received with thanksgiving needs to be rejected, because the word of God and prayer make it holy (1 Timothy 4:3–5).

Saul was not saying that anything edible is kosher. A closer look shows that he gave two criteria for defining what constitutes "food." One is prayer (i.e., the traditional Hebrew blessing). Observant Jews always make a *b'rachah* ("blessing") over foods before they are eaten. There are blessings for fruit, vegetables and a whole meal if bread is served. An example of one of these blessings is:

> *Barukh atah Adonai, eloheynu melekh ha'olam, ha'motzi lekhem min ha'aretz. Amen.*

> Blessed art Thou, O Lord our God, King of the universe who brings forth bread from the earth. Amen.

It is not enough to merely bless God in prayer *before* a meal, but in Jewish tradition it has always been important to bless God *after* the meal. This is based on the Torah injunction, "When you have eaten and are satisfied, praise the Lord your

God..." (Deuteronomy 8:10). This prayer, called *birkat ha' mazon* ("blessing over the meal") is much more detailed, about four or five pages long. It makes sense to chant the shorter prayer before eating and the longer one after a satisfying meal. Yeshua blessed God in this traditional way as he blessed the food. Although there is room for personal prayer, it seems more likely that Saul had this important Jewish custom in mind when he wrote to Timothy.

In defining the word "foods," not only are the blessings important but most significant is Saul's other measurement: the Word of God (verse 5). The false teachers spoken of in this passage seemed to question the *kashrut* of certain foods that were not prepared according to the rabbinic tradition. Saul responded by saying that the Scriptures are our final court of arbitration.

What about *kashrut* today? For Messianic Jews and Gentiles, if a food is listed in the Bible (e.g., Leviticus 11) and is thankfully received, it is kosher. Saul was not in any way implying that a prayer over pork or shellfish would render them kosher. One would be hard pressed to find a Hebrew blessing over either. This passage in 1 Timothy confirms what Yeshua had taught; the disciples should be more concerned about the spiritual lessons of *kashrut* than the rabbinic, extra-biblical details. Perhaps it is ironic that this verse expresses the very thing that the rabbis commonly called for in sanctifying a meal—the Torah and the blessings (see Buxbaum quote above).

There is freedom in the Messianic faith. However, that same freedom allows Yeshua's disciples to choose to follow and to appreciate the spiritual significance of *kashrut* (see Leviticus 11:45; Mark 7). It is a diet that reminds one of their holy calling from the Messiah. Secondly, it should not be overlooked that there are physical benefits to observing the dietary laws. There is an old joke in which a confused believer, having studied *kashrut*, asks his Messianic congregational leader: "Do you mean to say a little bacon will keep me out of heaven?" "On the contrary," the teacher replied. "You may get there even quicker!"

To have a kosher heart and life are the higher priorities of God. Even so, it all comes down to the important guiding principle of the New Testament: "For the Kingdom of God is not eating and drinking, but righteousness, shalom and joy in the *Ruach HaKodesh*" (Romans 14:17).

PRACTICAL GUIDE FOR MESSIANIC KASHRUT OBSERVANCE

Much of what has been discussed in the traditional approach to *kashrut* may be applied to a Messianic Jewish lifestyle. A distinctive factor is the freedom that believers have in the *Ruakh HaKodesh* to prayerfully apply certain customs. As with the traditional Jewish community, there is also a great deal of diversity among believers in Yeshua when it comes to *kashrut*. Many follow what might be described as a "biblical kosher" approach. This lifestyle shows deference to the biblical dietary laws. Hence, only kosher animals are eaten; the *tareyf* animals are avoided. Pork, shellfish and the unclean fish listed in Leviticus 11 are avoided.

A question is often raised as to what to do with the extra-biblical customs the rabbis have included. There is a broad consensus, considering the teachings of the New Testament, that Messianic believers are not *bound* by the traditions of man. The mixing of milk and meat, for example, while an Orthodox Jewish tradition, is not a biblical law. This means that the laws pertaining to separate dishes, silverware and pots are really not an issue in seeking to live a biblical lifestyle. Of course, there are those who may choose to follow elements of rabbinic tradition. This is fine as long as it does not contradict Scripture and is done in the right spirit.

A Messianic believer may want to buy meat from a kosher butcher and/or keep separate dishes. Some believers may prefer some modifications. Whatever approach a Messianic believer takes to *kashrut*, it is wise to walk in love and to heed the New Testament's council: "whatever you do, whether it's eating or drinking or anything else, do it all so as to bring glory to God" (1 Corinthians 10:31).

8

Mikveh

Ritual Water Immersion

THE HISTORICAL BACKGROUND

The LORD said to Moses, "These are the regulations for the diseased person at the time of his ceremonial cleansing, when he is brought to the priest: The priest is to go outside the camp and examine him. If the person has been healed of his infectious skin disease, the priest shall order that two live clean birds and some cedar wood, scarlet yarn and hyssop be brought for the one to be cleansed. . . . Seven times he shall sprinkle the one to be cleansed of the infectious disease and pronounce him clean. . . . He must wash his clothes and bathe himself with water, and he will be clean" (Leviticus 14:1–4, 7, 9).

Baptism sounds like such a non-Jewish concept, *oy vey* (oh my)! Most people jump to this conclusion based on the last two thousand years of church history. However, as with so many other aspects of Christianity, virtually everything goes back to its Jewish roots. Some may find it difficult to make the connection between baptism and Jewish customs, but the historical facts are irrefutable.

Much of the confusion derives from the word itself, baptism. *Baptidzo* is actually the Greek equivalent for the Hebrew *t'vilah* ("to totally immerse"). The concept of ceremonial washings is as old as the Torah itself. God commanded the Hebrew people to wash their clothing before he gave them the Law at Mt. Sinai (see Exodus 19:10). In Leviticus, chapters 8 and 16, Aaron and his sons were commanded to wash before they ministered in the Tabernacle. There were ritual cleansings for various flows of body fluids, such as a women's menstrual period (see Leviticus 15). Perhaps the most instructional passage in the Torah about *t'vilah* is in the quoted passage above dealing with the healing of leprosy.

This awful skin disease was the most dreaded of its day. It was the incurable plague that left the sufferer at the mercy of God. However, when God performed the miraculous and a leper was healed, the described ceremony took place. Designated sacrifices were brought to the Tabernacle or Temple, after it was confirmed by the priest that a true healing had taken place. It is noteworthy that the person was *immersed* in water after the healing was validated. Obviously, this was not meant for physical cleansing. Since this immersion took place after the healing, it clearly signifies a spiritual cleansing.

While it was always possible to have this immersion in a body of fresh water such as a lake or river, it became a common practice to have a special pool constructed, called a *mikveh*. The name is derived from the Hebrew word for "collection or gathering" and speaks of a place where the waters of the immersion are gathered. The earliest biblical usage for the specific word *mikveh* is found in Genesis 1:9, where God called for the collection of the waters during the creation week. In 1 Kings 7:23ff, it is pointed out that Solomon had constructed two thousand "baths" for the priesthood to carry out their duties in the first Temple. Recent discoveries in Israel have found many *mikve'ot* (plural of *mikveh*) in the archeological digs of the second Temple compound. Similarly, it has been found that the Qumran community (i.e., the Essenes) not only wrote about the importance of *t'vilah*, but they also built many *mikve'ot* in the Judean desert (Connolly, *Living in the Time of Jesus of Nazareth*, p. 31).

The practice of *mikveh* was quite common in the second Temple period, as shown by the large number of references to this custom in the Talmud. The ritual immersions for healings and service continued as prescribed by the Torah. However, especially interesting is the practice of *t'vilah* for Gentile converts to Judaism. According to the discussions of the Talmud, this custom had been instituted some time before the first century. The two main schools of rabbinic thought, *beyt* Shammai ("house of Shammai") and *beyt* Hillel ("house of Hillel"), debated the requirements for non-Jews to join Israel. While Shammai stressed the priority of circumcision, Hillel argued that *mikveh* was more important because it symbolized repentance and spiritual cleansing. Maimonides built upon this analogy of the *mikveh* (Birnbaum, *Mishneh Torah*, Mikva'ot 11:12) by applying it to the verse in Ezekiel that speaks of new spiritual life:

> I will sprinkle clean water on you, and you will be clean; I will cleanse you from all your impurities and from all your idols (Ezekiel 36:25).

Indeed, the waters of the *mikveh* still hold rich spiritual lessons for those who would take a closer look at this custom appointed by God.

TRADITIONAL JEWISH OBSERVANCE

The practice of the *mikveh* is still followed by traditional Jews to this day. There are some notable changes from ancient practice since the destruction of the Temple in 70 C.E. With that traumatic event, many of the laws in the Bible were considered obsolete. The sacrificial system was gone, and the priests had no place to serve. With the Temple destroyed, Rabbinic Judaism was forced to adjust biblical teachings in order to accommodate the new reality facing the Jewish people. Their conclusion, after much debate, was to substitute prescribed prayers and righteous works for the biblical requirement of sacrifice.

With the destruction of the Temple, the custom of *mikveh* changed, too. The cleansings for the priests and the related healings were no longer practical. However, modern Judaism maintained the need for *mikveh* in some situations. One is for the cleansing of a woman through the purification of the *niddah* (literally "removed or separated"), after her menstrual period. The Torah specifies that a woman shall be separated from her husband for seven days at this time of the month, abstaining from sexual relations (Leviticus 15:19–24). The rabbis commonly interpreted this to mean seven days from the end of her period; hence, a total of about twelve days. After those days, a Jewish woman is to go to a local *mikveh*. However, before immersion, she must meticulously bathe herself to remove even the smallest speck of dirt. Only then can she take the full immersion in the *mikveh*. Immersion is clearly intended for spiritual purification, since it occurs *after* the cleansing bath. Orthodox men will also immerse in the *mikveh* in spiritual preparation for the *shabbat* or for one of the holy days.

Another modern use of the *mikveh* is for the immersion of Gentiles who wish to convert to Rabbinic Judaism. The details of how this is done vary from group to group, but most are agreed that this ceremony is needed to ensure the reality of the conversion. After a series of studies, usually including Hebrew and Jewish customs, the new convert is required to be fully immersed in the waters of a kosher *mikveh*. Since it is considered important that every part of the body be immersed in the water, a normal *t'vilah* ceremony usually takes place in a private bath house. A loose garment may be worn for modesty reasons, and the immersion should be witnessed by a member of the same sex.

The following blessings are recited after the person immerses himself or herself one time:

Barukh atah Adonai, eloheynu melekh ha'olam, asher kidshanu b'mitzvotav v'tzivanu al ha-t'vilah.

Blessed art Thou, O Lord our God, King of the universe who has sanctified us by his commandments and commanded us concerning the ritual immersion.

In the case of a new convert to Rabbinic Judaism, an extra blessing is added:

Barukh atah Adonai, eloheynu melekh ha'olam, shehekheyanu v'kiymanu v'higiyanu lazman ha'zeh.

Blessed are Thou, O Lord our God, King of the universe who has kept us in life, sustained us and brought us to this time.

The fact that the Hebrew blessings are said after the act of immersion of the convert is unusual. Normally a blessing is said before any act of obedience. However, the convert cannot technically recite the blessing until after his immersion because he is not yet a Jew.

The Bible says little about the actual construction of a *mikveh*. However, what the Bible leaves undefined, the rabbis have elucidated in great detail. Among the many precepts stressed by rabbinic tradition is that the *mikveh* must contain either rain water or water from a natural spring or stream. There must be enough of this pure water for the full immersion of a person (i.e., about 120 gallons, as a minimum). Additional water from piped sources may be used if this minimum requirement has been met. Due to these technicalities, there are various interpretations on how to construct a *mikveh*. Traditional Jews are very concerned that the piping system and the actual pool meet the requirements of *halakhah* ("traditional Law") (Klein, A *Guide to Jewish Religious Practice*, p. 518ff).

Because of the similarities between a swimming pool and a traditional *mikveh*, the modern question has arisen as to whether the swimming pool is just as acceptable. Rabbinic authorities are split on this question, with some saying that a pool is acceptable if there is no other ritual *mikveh* available. Similar questions arise as one considers a river, lake or ocean for an immersion. While these contain the fresh water required, they are not often used because of the rabbi's opinion that a *mikveh* must be a permanently built structure, and for modesty reasons. However, rivers, lakes and oceans are acceptable when a permanent *mikveh* structure is not available in the community.

Despite all the tedious details, one should not lose sight of the *mikveh's* meaning. The Bible draws a distinction between the holy and the profane, between the clean and unclean. The waters of the *mikveh*, according to the rabbis, teach the Jewish people a great deal concerning these truths. The *niddah* period is to teach husbands and wives the need for discipline, respect and moderation in all things. The waters symbolize spiritual cleansing, as seen in the *mikveh* for Gentile converts to Rabbinic Judaism. For traditional Jews, the ritual immersion is also a graphic reminder of their need for God's cleansing and new life. As one source notes:

> One interpretation of the mikveh relates it to an experience of death and resurrection, and also to the reentry into the womb and reemergence. Immersing fully, you are like the fetus in the womb, and when you come up out of the mikveh you are as reborn. The individual who has sinned and become impure is transformed; he dies and is resurrected and becomes a new creation, like a newborn child (Buxbaum, *Jewish Spiritual Practices*, p. 569).

These thoughts may sound familiar to those who remember Yeshua's dialogue with a certain rabbi (see John 3), as well as Saul's description of the Messianic *mikveh* (Romans 6). With this understanding of the *mikveh*, it should become more meaningful. The *mikveh* can be appreciated as a beautiful custom appointed by God to remind all of the need for new spiritual life and a pure walk in this world.

RELEVANCE TO THE NEW TESTAMENT

As previously mentioned, baptism sounds foreign to the Jewish ear; yet the concept comes entirely from the ancient Jewish practice of *mikveh*. Water baptism is not therefore something "Gentile," or even pagan. Therefore, both Gentile Christian and Jew should look back at the historical reality of *mikveh*. As one reads the New Testament's teaching concerning water immersion, Christianity's connection to its Jewish roots becomes more obvious.

The most prominent example of *t'vilah* in the New Testament is found in the early chapters of the Gospels. There was a prophet in that generation who practiced *t'vilah* as an integral part of his ministry, and was therefore known as *Yokhanan* the Immerser ("John the Baptizer").

> It was during those days that Yochanan the Immerser arrived in the desert of Y'hudah and began proclaiming the message, "Turn from your sins to God, for the Kingdom of Heaven is near!" This is the man Yesha'yahu [Isaiah] was talking about when he said,
>   The voice of someone crying out:
>   'In the desert prepare the way of Adonai!
>   Make straight paths for him!
> Yochanan wore clothes of camel's hair with a leather belt around his waist, and his food was locusts and wild honey. People went out to him from Yerushalayim, from all Y'hudah, and from the whole region around the Yarden [Jordan]. Confessing their sins, they were immersed by him in the Yarden River (Matthew 3:1–6).

This account matches many of the details already known about *mikveh* and its significance in the Jewish culture. *Yokhanan* was sent to prepare the way for Messiah. In so doing, he preached the message: turn and repent. From the chronological studies of the Gospels, it is believed by many that this event took place in the fall of the year. This message (i.e., *T'shuvah!* "Repent!") is a familiar one for Jewish people during that time of year (i.e., during the High Holy Days). The Jewish

New Year (*Rosh Hashanah*) is the most focused time of year, where Israel assesses her spiritual condition and turns back to God (Kasdan, *God's Appointed Times*, p. 66).

Assuming that *Yokhanan* was preaching at the time of *Rosh Hashanah*, it is consistent to think that the Jewish men would naturally consider taking a *mikveh*. To this day, men still immerse in the *mikveh*. This is a sign of their inward cleansing as they spiritually prepare for the Holy Days. This was even more true for those traditional Jews who were receiving *Yokhanan's* exhortation to be ready for the coming Messiah. They identified with his message and took the sign of cleansing through the *mikveh* in the Jordan River.

The custom of *mikveh* becomes increasingly important as one studies the pages of the New Testament. Saul of Tarsus was certainly no stranger to the *mikveh* and its spiritual lessons. He drew strongly on these lessons as he taught the Messianic believers in Rome about their faith-walk with Yeshua. In describing the reality of their salvation, he wrote:

> Don't you know that those of us who have been immersed into the Messiah Yeshua have been immersed into his death? Through immersion into his death we were buried with him; so that just as, through the glory of the Father, the Messiah was raised from the dead, likewise we too might live a new life (Romans 6:3–4).

The spiritual lessons of the Jewish *mikveh* perfectly picture what God has done for the believer in the Messiah. Believers have been buried, as it were, with Yeshua and raised up by his resurrection power. Some of the finer details of the *mikveh* should also be noted to help in understanding these truths.

For much of church history there have been debates on just what manner of baptism is best. Should it be dipping, sprinkling or pouring? It seems that these debates are all academic as one looks back to the Jewish roots of baptism, as found in the *mikveh*. There is no doubt as to the mode used in the *mikveh*. It is full and total immersion, so that all the body makes contact with the water.

This seems to best fit Saul's teaching on the significance of water immersion in the New Testament. While there is freedom in the Ruakh Ha'Kodesh to adjust some of the traditions and customs of the Bible (especially if a person is physically unable to go into the water), it is rather apparent that full immersion best illustrates the truth of Romans 6. What better way to show that believers have been buried with Messiah than to actually go under the water. In addition, the coming up out of the water provides a graphic representation of being raised up with Yeshua.

Not surprisingly, the mikveh continued to be very significant throughout the Gospel accounts, even to the last message of Yeshua. As he was commissioning his disciples to their new work, he said:

> All authority in heaven and on earth has been given to me. Therefore, go and make people from all nations into talmidim, immersing them into the reality of the Father, the Son and the Ruach Ha'Kodesh, and teaching them to obey everything that I have commanded you. And remember! I will be with you always, yes, even until the end of the age (Matthew 28:18–20).

Shortly after the resurrection of Yeshua, mention is made of what might be called the "Messianic mikveh." On the day of Shavuot (Pentecost), as recorded in Acts 2, thousands of Jewish people had gathered to celebrate the feast After the outpouring of the Ruakh HaKodesh on the Messianic remnant, Shim'on gave his powerful message about the messiahship of Yeshua. The wonderful results were the salvation of three thousand Jewish people at one time. These new disciples now had a logistical problem. In obedience to the command of Yeshua, these new believers were exhorted to receive the mikveh as a sign of their faith commitment. It is normally assumed that all these events took place in "the upper room" of Yeshua's last Passover seder. However, it is impossible that thousands of people could gather in such a room, and that three thousand new believers could be immersed in water there.

A closer look at Acts 2 shows that these events did not occur in the "upper room," but at "one place" later described as "the whole house" (verses 1–2). In Hebrew, there is another place called a "house" (*bayit*), namely the Holy Temple (*Beyt Ha'Mikdash*). The fact is that these events took place in the public area of the Temple compound, where such multitudes could easily gather. This would likewise explain the ease in which the three thousand new believers received the *mikveh* in Yeshua's name. Modern archaeological digs have confirmed that there were indeed dozens of *mikve'ot* in the courts of the Temple during the time of Yeshua. It is appropriate that what was often used for various immersions by Jewish worshippers was used on *Shavuot* to illustrate the spiritual cleansing of those who believed that the Messiah had come.

The New Testament confirms virtually all the customs of the Hebrew Scriptures, including the spiritual importance of the waters of the *mikveh*. It does not confer salvation but, as with the example of the healed person in Leviticus, it is a wonderful symbol of a healing that has already taken place. *Shim'on*, in his letter to some Jewish believers, summarized the significance of this Messianic under-standing of the *mikveh*:

> This also prefigures what delivers us now, the water of immersion, which is not the removal of dirt from the body, but one's pledge to keep a good conscience toward God, through the resurrection of Yeshua the Messiah (1 Peter 3:21).

PRACTICAL GUIDE FOR A MESSIANIC MIKVEH SERVICE

Due to its rich symbolism and because it was a command from Messiah (see Matthew 28:19), believers in Yeshua follow this custom of immersion in the *mikveh*. Salvation is secured by trusting in the Messiah's death and resurrection (see Ephesians 2:8–9). However, the Messianic *mikveh*, a sign of what God has done for believers, is an important testimony of one's faith. One should not overlook the fact that a Messianic *mikveh* will often serve as a public testimony to the world that there is a growing remnant of Jews and Gentiles who call on Messiah's name.

Most Messianic *mikve'ot* take place at swimming pools, rivers or oceans. Modest dress is appropriate for such an occasion, perhaps a swimming suit with a cover-up. There are varying customs in regard to *mikveh*, so these may also vary among Messianic groups. Some traditions simply have the participants immerse themselves within the sight of witnesses. These witnesses will assist the person in the process of the actual immersion. Whatever the details in the procedure, the important thing is to follow Yeshua's command to illustrate his spiritual reality in one's life.

This ceremony is simple yet powerful. A wonderful part of the event can be having the person share a personal testimony of how they found Messiah. A Messianic immersion service can take place at any time. At *Kehilat Ariel* Messianic Congregation (this author's congregation), the *mikveh* is observed at two key times of the year. On the afternoon of *Rosh Hashanah*, there is a ceremony of repentance called *tashlikh* that takes place at a body of water. This is the perfect context for a Messianic *mikveh* service. The second *mikveh* service takes place shortly after Passover, as believers reflect on their redemption. Appropriate Scripture readings and music can also enhance this joyful time. As the people are immersed, the traditional blessings can be recited with some Messianic adaptations:

Barukh atah Adonai, eloheynu melekh ha'olam, asher kidshanu b'mitzvotav v'tzivunu ul ha-t'vilah (one can add: b'shem Ha'Av, Yeshua HaMashiakh v'Ruakh HaKodesh). Amen.

Blessed art Thou, O Lord our God, King of the universe who has sanctified us by his commandments and commanded us concerning the immersion (in the name of the Father, Yeshua the Messiah and the Holy Spirit). Amen.

Barukh atah Adonai, eloheynu melekh ha'olam, shehekheyanu v'kiymanu v'higiyanu lazman ha'zeh. Amen.

Blessed art Thou, O Lord our God, King of the universe who has given us life, sustained us and brought us to this time. Amen.

Every person needs to ask if he or she has found the new life illustrated in the waters of the *mikveh*. Every believer needs to take the sign (i.e., immersion in a *mikveh*) of their salvation in Yeshua the Messiah. May this God-appointed custom be a source of great joy for those who have been touched by the power of the living God.

9

Tzitziyot

The Fringes

THE HISTORICAL BACKGROUND

The LORD said to Moses, "Speak to the Israelites and say to them: 'Throughout the generations to come you are to make tassels on the corners of your garments, with a blue cord on each tassel. You will have these tassels to look at and so you will remember all the commands of the LORD, that you may obey them and not prostitute yourselves by going after the lusts of your own hearts and eyes. Then you will remember to obey all my commands and will be consecrated to your God. I am the LORD your God, who brought you out of Egypt to be your God. I am the LORD your God'" (Numbers 15:37–41).

One of the more identifiably Jewish customs is that of the fringes worn on certain garments. To this day, Orthodox Jews display the fringes as a sign of their devotion to God and as a means of identifying with their people. Where did this unusual custom originate, and what was the meaning of it to earlier generations?

The command to wear fringes is directly from God. He wanted Israel to be constantly reminded that they were a distinct people, set-apart for service to the one true God. Therefore, the holy days, worship style and diet reflected spiritual truth. Even the clothing of the Jew reminded him of his special calling. The *tzitzit* ("fringe," "fringed garment" or "tassel") was a clear marker in the world that Israel had a God-ordained mission. The biblical command is clear. Israel was told to wear the *tzitziyot* (plural of *tzitzit*) on the corners of their outer garments. Jewish tradition adds many additional details concerning the essence and use of the *tzitziyot*.

The construction of the fringes has a special tradition and significance. Each corner of the outer garment was to have one long thread that was dyed a special shade of blue, a reminder of the sky and Israel's heavenly focus. This long thread was connected to three shorter threads, making a total of four threads for each corner of the garment. These fringes were tied in such a manner so as to double them, so that they would total eight strands. These strands were tied in a series of five double knots to symbolically represent the number thirteen. Interestingly, by adding this number to the numerical value (in Hebrew) of the word *tzitzit* (i.e., 600), one arrives at a total of 613. This is the number of commandments contained in the Torah. Hence, the purpose of the *tzitziyot* are clearly fulfilled each time they remind a traditional Jew to follow *all* of God's commandments.

As noted in an earlier chapter, the *tzitziyot*, which represent the Jew's obligation to follow the commandments, are rendered invalid upon death. To symbolize this, the fringes are cut off the *tallit* ("prayer shawl"). This provides an interesting insight into the historical situation during the time of King David. At one point, David was able to sneak up on his sleeping pursuer, King Saul, and cut off the edge of his robe. This was clearly symbolic of death, yet David felt remorseful and still encouraged his men to spare Saul's life (see 1 Samuel 24).

Not only were the *tzitziyot* a reminder to follow God's ways, they were also a statement of who God is. This can be seen from the fact that each fringe had 39 windings, corresponding to the numerical value of the Hebrew phrase *Adonai Ekhad* ("The LORD is One"). Ancient Israel lived in a world surrounded by paganism and false gods. This custom must have been a graphic reminder that the Jewish people were not to follow the broad path to destruction but the narrow path of life in the one true God. Every part of life for the Jew, even the way he dressed, was to somehow remind him of these realities.

TRADITIONAL JEWISH OBSERVANCE

The custom of *tzitziyot* is still followed today by traditional Jews, with some slight modifications from the biblical command. The most obvious adaptation for most Jews is that the *tzitziyot* are not worn as a part of the regular garments. Instead of the tassels on the corners of the tunic or outer garment, Jewish tradition developed the custom of the *tallit*. This special garment is usually worn in synagogue or during special worship occasions. It contains the same series of fringes and knots on its four corners and is often embroidered with Judaic artwork. This biblical custom underwent some changes, most notably during the Middle Ages, when Jews were scattered throughout the Gentile world. Wearing the fringes on their personal garments would have meant subjecting themselves to persecution and danger. Therefore, the custom was modified so that the fringes were mainly worn in the synagogue. Orthodox Jews, today, feel that they still fulfill the spirit of the commandment by wearing an undergarment that carries the fringes—*tallit katan* ("small prayer shawl"). This garment is worn during all waking hours.

For most Jews, this *mitzvah* is fulfilled in the prayer shawl, worn only at religious services. Since the rabbis note that this commandment states that "you will look at them," it is inter-

preted that this custom is only required in daylight hours. Hence, the *tallit* (or *tallis* in Ashkenazi Hebrew) is not usually worn at night, even in the synagogue, except perhaps by the rabbi or cantor leading the services. Likewise, women are not obligated to wear the fringes at any time because the rabbis say they are exempt from any commands that are time related.

Due to the importance of this custom, it is quite common to see Jewish men wearing the *tallit* at daytime synagogue services. There are often extra prayer shawls made available in the lobby for visitors. Before placing the *tallit* on one's shoulders, it is held with both hands and the Hebrew blessing is recited:

Barukh atah Adonai, eloheynu melekh ha'olam, asher kidshanu b'mitzvotav v'tzivanu l'hit'ateyf ba'tzitzit.

Blessed art Thou, O Lord our God, King of the universe who has sanctified us by his commandments and commanded us to wrap ourselves in the fringes.

If a person is blessing the *tallit katan* prior to putting it on, the following is said:

Barukh atah Adonai, eloheynu melekh ha'olam, asher kidshanu b'mitzvotav v'tzivanu al mitzvat tzitzit.

Blessed art Thou, O Lord our God, King of the universe who has sanctified us by his commandments and commanded us concerning the command of the fringes.

The modern *tallit* can have a number of designs and artistic handiwork. However, one traditional element is noticeably missing; that is, the thread of blue prescribed by the Torah. Why is blue thread not used? As with so many other traditions of the Bible, this custom changed after the destruction of the Jerusalem Temple. Without a functioning priesthood and service, the blue dye and thread fell into disuse and were eventually forgotten. Part of the problem was the expense and rarity of the blue dye. Known as *t'kheylet* in Hebrew, the exact shade of blue extracted from a Mediterranean sea snail was uncertain.

This became a moot point in the Middle Ages, as the snail disappeared from the shores of Israel. Curiously, within recent years the sea snail has been reappearing. This has so excited some Orthodox groups, specifically a group called the Temple Institute, that they have developed a renewed process for extracting this dye. They plan for the *t'kheylet* to be part of the priestly garments for use in the rebuilt Temple.

Through all the long history of Israel, the words of the Torah have proven true. To this day, the *tzitziyot* remind Israel that God has consecrated the Jewish people to himself. It seems that in the last days even the nations will have a greater appreciation of God's covenant with the Jewish people. In seeking the faith of the God of Israel, many non-Jews will reach out in a rather unusual way:

> This is what the LORD Almighty says: "In those days ten men from all languages and nations will take firm hold of one Jew by the hem of his robe and say, 'Let us go with you, because we have heard that God is with you'" (Zechariah 8:23).

RELEVANCE TO THE NEW TESTAMENT

Considering the importance of the custom of *tzitziyot*, one would expect to find some significant references in the New Testament. The fringes have always been the most obvious identifying mark of the Jewish community. Since Yeshua and all his disciples were traditional Jews, one can assume that they followed this command of the Torah.

The Gospel of Matthew provides an account of Yeshua observing this commandment. The word had spread throughout Israel that a great rabbi and healer had come. Multitudes of people sought his touch, thinking this might even be the long-awaited Messiah. Matthew's account describes the healing that took place.

> A woman who had had a hemorrhage for twelve years approached him from behind and touched the tzitzit on his robe. For she said to herself, "If I can only touch his robe, I will be healed." Yeshua turned, saw her and said, "Courage, daughter! Your trust has healed you." And she was instantly healed (Matthew 9:20–22).

Upon reading this passage, one might rashly judge this woman for acting on superstition. Why was she so concerned with mere external things? Did she think there was some kind of power associated with the fringes themselves? As one reflects on the meaning of the *tzitziyot* in Judaism, one can see a different side to her actions.

The tassels on the corners of the garments reminded the Jews of their call to the Word of God. The Jewish people were actually representatives of the one, true God. The fact that this suffering woman reached out to the *tzitziyot* of the Messiah was actually a statement of faith, not superstition. This suffering woman's reaching out to the healing power of God was an indicator of her spiritual condition. It is not surprising that Yeshua validated her action. One should not miss the obvious fact that Yeshua himself wore the *tzitziyot* as commanded by the Torah. If anyone ever exemplified the perfect, spirit-led Jew, who walked in obedience to the Torah, it was Yeshua of Natzeret.

As with any custom or tradition, there is always the danger that it can be distorted beyond its original meaning. This same Yeshua, who wore *tzitziyot*, gave his Jewish disciples a word of warning regarding the traditions. In exposing the hypocrisy of some of the Pharisees, Yeshua said that they love to be seen by others, so they "make their *t'fillin* broad and their *tzitziyot* long" (Matthew 23:5). Clearly Yeshua was not universally condemning the use of the fringes, or he himself would stand condemned. What he was condemning was not the use of *tzitziyot*, but the abuse of this important command of God. Too often, people lose perspective on the spiritual lessons of a custom and substitute their own confused ideas. Yeshua was rightly pointing out the inconsistency of having kosher *tzitziyot* without having a kosher heart. It is the height of irony that the biblical custom that was meant to remind the Jew to keep his eyes on God would actually be used to exalt self. As was so often the case, Yeshua taught his people concerning the original spiritual understanding of the Law and customs (see Matthew 5:17).

PRACTICAL GUIDE FOR A MESSIANIC PRACTICE OF TZITZIYOT

As a custom based directly on the Word of God, *tzitziyot* may be joyfully worn today by followers of Yeshua. As with the larger Jewish community, there are a variety of practices of this custom among Messianic Jews and Gentiles. There are some who feel called to maintain a daily expression of the fringes that requires the wearing of the *tallit katan* ("small prayer shawl"). With the right focus and attitude, this can be a very meaningful expression of faith. More often, Messianic Jews follow the common approach of wearing the regular *tallit* at religious services or special occasions. Many Messianic congregations provide extra *tallitot* for visitors at their *shabbat* services. Since the age of thirteen is considered the age of accountability, where boys are required to observe the commandments for themselves, it is a beautiful gesture to give a *tallit* as a gift at a Bar Mitzvah. This is often done as a gift from the congregation or the *shabbat* school.

What about women and the practice of *tzitziyot*? The older tradition is that women are exempt from this time-bound commandment. Modern Conservative and even Reform synagogues have increasingly allowed women to wear the *tallit* in their services. While there is nothing forbidding women to wear a *tallit* at worship services, the author of this book tends to agree with the older practice of men being the only ones responsible for this custom.

The same questions could be asked in regard to Gentile believers in Yeshua. Is it only Jews who can benefit from donning the *tallit*? Saul of Tarsus stated that the non-Jew who believes in Messiah is grafted into the same rich olive tree as the Jewish believer (see Romans 11). The non-Jews also enjoy the spiritual blessings purchased by the Messiah. If a Gentile believer chooses to wear a *tallit*, this can be a beautiful statement of his faith in the God of Israel. In a Messianic Jewish worship service, such a practice can be a positive testimony of the Gentile believer's stand with the Jewish people (see 1 Corinthians 9:19–20). Once again, it is a question of personal conviction that must be sincere. However, care should be taken not to confuse the issue by thinking that a *tallit* is going to transform a Gentile into a Jew.

Regarding the details of the *tallit*, there is freedom in the areas of artistic design and use. The important symbolism is the *tzitziyot* on the corners of the garment. All else is secondary and open to personal taste. Similarly, the traditional blessing said before wearing the *tallit* (see above) is quite appropriate for any Messianic believer. May the custom of *tzitziyot* and *tallit* be rich reminders to all believers in Messiah to stay focused on his word and to honor God with every part of their lives.

10

 **Kippah**

The Headcovering

THE HISTORICAL BACKGROUND

Have Aaron your brother brought to you from among the Israelites, along with his sons Nadab and Abihu, Eleazar and Ithamar, so they may serve me as priests. Make sacred garments for your brother Aaron, to give him dignity and honor. Tell all the skilled men to whom I have given wisdom in such matters that they are to make garments for Aaron, for his consecration, so he may serve me as priest. These are the garments they are to make: a breastpiece, an ephod, a robe, a woven tunic, a turban and a sash. They are to make these sacred garments for your brother Aaron and his sons, so they may serve me as priests (Exodus 28:1–4).

From the days of Moses, one of the distinguishing marks of the Jewish people has been the headcovering. Traditional Jewish women often have their heads covered with a scarf or even a wig. Orthodox men are always seen wearing some kind of headcovering, whether it be a skullcap or a traditional hat. Most Jewish men, no matter what branch they are affiliated with, will wear the headcovering when attending a Jewish place of worship.

Where did this custom come from? The concept of a headcovering was actually formalized with the priestly garments of Israel. God was careful to make it clear to Moses that the people needed to have mediators in order to have communion with him. The God of Israel is holy and pure beyond description, whereas mankind has fallen away from God because of its sin (see Habakkuk 1:13). Today, some question the need for mediators in their relationship with God. Others think that the concept of a priesthood is useless. However, it is really a gift of grace from God that he established as a way for Israel to commune with him, even in their unrighteous state.

The *Cohanim* (sons of Aaron) and the *Levi'im* (tribe of Levi) were the ones appointed as these priests. They were to represent God to the people, but also the people to God. Such a holy service was not to be taken lightly, and called for special garments. Among this holy attire was the turban. The Hebrew word *mitznefet* comes from the root "to wrap," implying that this was a miter or a turban-style of headcovering.

What did this turban symbolize? The same chapter of Exodus states that the headcovering of the priest was to be embellished with the words "HOLY TO THE LORD" (Exodus 28:36–38). Clearly, this *mitznefet* was to be a reminder that God is characterized by the attribute of moral perfection.

Although this custom was originally applicable only to the priesthood, later in history the larger Jewish community began to wear headcoverings. The assumption was that if the priests were required to cover their heads, then it would be appropriate for all men to wear this sign of submission.

It was a custom to cover one's head as a sign of mourning, as described in 2 Samuel 15:30. Later, Jewish tradition regarded a man with an uncovered head as indecent or even pagan. So important was the headcovering that some of the talmudic rabbis spoke of not walking even six steps without the proper head attire (*Babylonian Talmud*, Kiddushin 31a). Another talmudic discussion noted that a man should have his head covered to show "humility in prayer" (*Babylonian Talmud*, Rosh Hashanah 17b). Perhaps the best summary statement on the reasons for the headcovering is so that "the fear of God will be upon you" (*Babylonian Talmud*, Shabbat 156b). This brings to mind the old Hebrew National hot-dog commercial, which states that they "answer to a higher authority." The headcovering is a reminder to Israel that there is *someone* watching over them.

It might surprise some to note that there has not always been a uniform practice of wearing headcoverings. As common as the custom has become in recent history, there have been many times where the wearing of such a garment was not followed. Some rabbis disagreed with the practice, so the headcovering was not worn by all men (*Babylonian Talmud*, Kiddushin 29b). In addition, the rabbis stated that the wearing of a headcovering was "optional and a matter of custom" (*Babylonian Talmud*, Nedarim 30b). This diversity of opinion is seen in pictures and inscriptions in which some Jewish men are wearing the headcovering while others are not. Therefore, the wearing of a headcovering was by no means universally accepted until late in Jewish history, about 1700 C.E.

Over the last 300 years, traditional Jews have been well known for wearing hats or some other type of headcovering. In some European communities, the hat was transformed into the smaller *yarmulke* (Yiddish)/ *kippah* (Hebrew). It has been noted that the word *yarmulke* may even provide the reason for having one's head covered, as it might be an acronym for the Hebrew expression *yirey m'Elohim* (the "fear of God"). Whatever form the headcovering may take, the lesson is clear: Jews are to always walk in submission and humility before the God who is always watching over them.

TRADITIONAL JEWISH OBSERVANCE

As one can see from this brief historical overview, the practice of the headcovering has taken on many different

expressions. More recently, the Orthodox Jews have in-
sisted on always having the head covered. A hat is quite
common, and it is often a distinguishing mark of the
particular sect of Orthodox Judaism that one is following.
Even with a hat, most will wear a *kippah*. Orthodox Jewish
women also continue the custom of having their heads
covered. In the Scriptures, the hair of the woman is considered to have special beauty, so they believe it must be
reserved for their husband alone (see Song of Songs 4:1).
Hence, married women from this group usually employ
either a special wig, called a *sheitel*, or a scarf.

Although the Orthodox Jews maintain this view, there
are other viewpoints espoused today by other branches
within Judaism. Con-
servative Jews agree
with the Orthodox that
men should wear a
kippah in synagogue or
while observing a
Jewish custom. How-
ever, they do not feel
an obligation to don
the headcovering at
all times. Reform
Jews take a liberal
view that the *kippah*
is never needed, although they may wear one on certain
occasions. Sometimes things can get very confusing, as
seen in a cartoon that appeared in an Israeli newspaper
depicting the Pope's visit with the President of Israel. The
caption read: "The Pope is the one with the Yarmulke"
(Rosten, *The Joys of Yiddish*, p. 428)! The debate on the
proper use of this custom will likely continue in the future
as it has through much of Jewish history.

RELEVANCE TO THE NEW TESTAMENT

One would expect this debate regarding headcoverings to
be brought up in yet another Jewish book, the New Testa-

ment. In his exhortation to the Messianic believers in Corinth, Saul of Tarsus presented some important guidelines for public worship services. Although he discussed such issues as spiritual gifts and love, Saul first addressed the subject of improper or confusing attire.

> Now I praise you because you have remembered everything I told you and observe the traditions just the way I passed them on to you. But I want you to understand that the head of every man is Messiah, and the head of a wife is her husband, and the head of the Messiah is God. Every man who prays or prophesies wearing something down over his head brings shame to his head, but every woman who prays or prophesies with her head unveiled brings shame to her head—there is no difference between her and a woman who has had her head shaved. For if a woman is not veiled, let her also have her hair cut short; but if it is shameful for a woman to wear her hair cut short or to have her head shaved, then let her be veiled (1 Corinthians 11:2–6).

In seeking to understand this much misunderstood passage, one should first note that Saul is evidently giving some counsel that is related to the culture of Corinth. The fact that he uses the word *traditions* is significant. The Greek word *paradosis* means that which is handed down from past generations. The Hebrew term equivalent to *paradosis* is *masoret*, and it speaks of those things handed down, whether biblical or extra biblical. There are good traditions (as seen in this passage and in 2 Thessalonians 2:15) and there are traditions that become bad by man-made distortions (as seen in Mark 7:3). It should not surprise anyone that Saul, addressing the question of attire for public worship, alluded to certain traditions. Even in the Jewish community, there has been debate about such customs. The intensity of the debate was much greater in the non-Jewish, pagan city of Corinth.

Saul admonished believers who came from a Greek culture to not cover their heads during prayer. Some believers today feel that this is a prohibition against the use of the *kippah* by modern Messianic Jews. However, Saul was clearly writing to those who were surrounded by the non-Jewish culture of Hellenism. Even for the Jews in Corinth, this directive probably did not present a conflict. The use or non-use of the *kippah* had been flexible, depending upon the particular culture where the Jewish people lived. The apostle seems to be referring to certain customs in Corinth that would bring confusion to the testimony of the Messianic believer (Edersheim, *Sketches of Jewish Social Life in the Days of Christ*, p. 154).

This was even more evident in Saul's exhortation to the women of Corinth. He told them to make sure that their heads were covered during public services. This was a common practice in cultures of the Middle East. However, there must have been something unusual taking place with the Corinthians. Evidently, there was a problem associated with women that had short hair or even shaved heads. Some commentators feel that this was a particular problem because such styles were associated with temple prostitution in pagan society (see A.T. Robertson, *Word Pictures in the New Testament*, Vol. IV, p. 160). In addition, the Jewish people often considered a shaved or uncovered head to be a sign of judgment (see Isaiah 7:20). It seems that Saul's concern was that these women who came out of pagan society should no longer identify with the gross immorality that was still practiced there. Saul required them to show their repentance and new life by not imitating the prevailing hair styles and, if necessary, by wearing a full veil.

Are these specific details to be applicable to every culture and community of Messianic believers? Although Saul was talking about *traditions*, he also gave some important principles for guidance in lifestyle decisions.

> For a man indeed should not have his head veiled, because he is the image and glory of God, and the woman is the glory of man. For man was not made from woman, but woman from man; and indeed man

was not created for the sake of the woman but woman for the sake of the man. The reason a woman should show by veiling her head that she is under authority has to do with the angels. Nevertheless, in union with the Lord neither is woman independent of man nor is man independent of woman; for as the woman was made from the man, so also the man is now born through the woman. But everything is from God (1 Corinthians 11:7–12).

Saul was giving the overriding principle to these exhortations concerning headcoverings. While there may be customs and traditions in society, it is always important to live in a way that honors biblical principles. What is the principle behind this passage? It is best summed up in Saul's phrase *under authority* (verse 10). The headcovering for the woman, or the *kippah* for the man, is really a secondary issue after the real issue of authority and submission. There is a God-ordained order for husband/wife relationships as well as the God/man relationship; hence, the mention of angels in verse ten. It was natural for Saul to bring up this problem in Corinth within the context of headcoverings, because this is the very issue that the *kippah* or scarf illustrated to the Jew. It is interesting that some of the modern Jewish cultural practices would have actually communicated the exact opposite of their intended purposes to the Greeks in Corinth. In much of Jewish history, the headcovering has actually emphasized the exact thing that Saul was encouraging in this passage, namely submission to God. Similarly, modern western society does not normally place a stigma of rebelliousness on women with short hair or men who cover their head. In light of these principles, it seems that the modern use of the *kippah* for men is not only acceptable but actually a fulfillment of what the apostle was teaching. Above all, the spirit by which any custom is observed is vital. Not surprisingly, it is in this same letter to the Corinthians that Saul exhorts them to focus their lifestyle on the principle of love (1 Corinthians 13). May all believers heed such wise counsel.

A PRACTICAL GUIDE FOR KIPPAH OR SCARF

By understanding some of the history of the *kippah* and headcoverings, one can better discern the place of these traditions in their personal lives. For those who feel that this custom fits the context of their Messianic faith, there is complete freedom to wear the *kippah*, and many will find it meaningful to do so. In practical terms, this may range from wearing a *kippah* at all waking hours to simply wearing one at services or in prayer. While there may be many areas of debate concerning traditions, believers in Yeshua must remember that they are to live their lives submitted to the God of Israel through the Messiah. In many church settings in various cultures, to cover one's head might confuse the issue of submission. However, in the modern Jewish culture, the *kippah* is consistent with the principle of submission to God. Considering Saul's philosophy of ministry, a Jewish or even Gentile believer who mingles with the Jewish community has good reason to follow this custom. Saul said that "with Jews, what I did was put myself in the position of a Jew, in order to win Jews" (1 Corinthians 9:20). The New Testament gives believers in Yeshua freedom in such nonessential issues, to follow or not to follow, depending on one's personal convictions (see Romans 14).

From the biblical perspective, the more important question is not whether one *wears* the sign of submission, but

whether one *lives* a life of submission. It does not benefit the believer to have a traditional outward expression coupled with a personal life that is out of God's order. Whatever one's practice, may all things be done for the sake of the love of Messiah. The *kippah* for men, or scarf for women, is a beautiful custom when properly understood. Believers in Yeshua need to ask themselves if they are walking in the truth that these customs are meant to communicate.

11

T'fillin

The Phylacteries

THE HISTORICAL BACKGROUND

So if you faithfully obey the commands I am giving you today—to love the Lord your God and to serve him with all your heart and with all your soul—when I will send rain on your land in its season, both autumn and spring rains, so that you may gather in your grain, new wine and oil. I will provide grass in the fields for your cattle, and you will eat and be satisfied. Be careful, or you will be enticed to turn away and worship other gods and bow down to them. Then the Lord's anger will burn against you, and he will shut the heavens so that it will not rain and the ground will yield no produce, and you will soon perish from the good land the Lord is giving you. Fix these words of mine in your hearts and minds; tie them as symbols on your hands and bind them on your foreheads. Teach them to your children, talking about them when you sit at home and when you walk along the road, when you lie down and when you get up. Write them on the doorframes of your houses and on your gates, so that your days and the days of your children may be many in the land that the LORD swore to give your forefathers, as many as the days that the heavens are above the earth (Deuteronomy 11:13–21).

One of the most ancient commands of the Scriptures is that the Hebrew people should tie certain reminders on their hands and foreheads. As with the *m'zuzah* on the door and the *tzitzit* on the garments, there were to be reminders of God's commands even on each person's body. However, the Bible is not expressly clear on how this is to be done. From ancient times, traditional Jews have fulfilled this commandment in the custom called *t'fillin*. The Hebrew word is related to the word for prayer (*t'fillah*) and provides the focus of this tradition. *T'fillin* were designed to provide practical helps for the prayer life of the Jew.

Over the generations, the *t'fillin* took the shape of leather boxes that were strapped to the forehead and to the hand. This type of *t'fillin* existed before the first century, as there are references to *t'fillin* in Jewish literature. Josephus, the Jewish historian, mentioned the use of *t'fillin* (Whiston, *Josephus' Complete Works*, Antiquities 4:213). One of the talmudic sages spoke of receiving the *t'fillin* handed down from his own grandfather (*Babylonian Talmud*, Sanhedrin 92b). The more recent discoveries of the Dead Sea Scrolls have also confirmed the fact that the Qumran community used many of their parchments for the custom of *t'fillin*.

Although there have been variations to this custom throughout the ages, the practice of *t'fillin* has remained remarkably unchanged for over two millennia. Some pious Jews of earlier days even wore the *t'fillin* constantly. However, the common practice today is for males over the age of thirteen to wear the leather boxes at daily morning (*shakharit*) services. By so doing, they are reminded that the commandments of God should be on their mind (forehead) and applied in their life (hand).

TRADITIONAL JEWISH OBSERVANCE

Jewish tradition developed two distinct parts to a set of t'fillin; *shel rosh* ("designated for the head") and *shel yad* ("designated for the hand"). *Shel rosh* consists of four individual compartments, each containing a parchment with handwritten passages from the Torah (Exodus 13:1–10, 11–16, Deuteronomy 6:4–9; 11:13–21). In contrast, *shel yad* is a single compartment that holds all of the same passages written on a single parchment. Why were these passages selected? They all have the common commandment to bind the Word of God on one's forehead and hand.

The symbolism of the knots should not be overlooked in the construction of the *t'fillin*. *Shel rosh* has the Hebrew letter *shin* on the outside of the box. The rabbis say that the knot tied on  the head-piece represents the Hebrew letter *dalet* and the end of the strap is the Hebrew letter *yod*. Together, the *shel rosh t'fillin* spells out the word *Shaddai* ("Almighty"). This same name of God is spelled out by the traditional wrappings of the leather strap for the *shel yad t'fillin*, thus reminding one that the object of their prayers is God.

Normally, *t'fillin* is not worn on the Sabbath, any holy day or at night. This is because of the fact that these other days are also called "signs" in the Scriptures and should not conflict with the sign of the *t'fillin*. The *t'fillin* is put on after the *tallit* ("prayer shawl"), to follow the rabbinic dictate that things that occur more often take precedent over things that occur less often (*Babylonian Talmud*, Z'vahim 89a). The *shel yad t'fillin* is applied first by wrapping it around the left arm, which is considered the weaker one. All jewelry should be removed from the arm first, and the shirt sleeve should be rolled up so that the straps are directly on the skin. It is also noted that the knot (*kesher*) of the *shel yad* on the left arm should be nearest to the heart. As the knot is tightened around the biceps, the following blessing is recited:

> *Barukh atah Adonai, eloheynu melekh ha' olam, asher kidshanu b' mitzvotav v' tzivanu l'haniakh t'fillin.*

Blessed art Thou, O Lord our God, King of the universe, who has sanctified us by His commandments and commanded us to put on t'fillin.

The leather arm strap is wound seven times around the forearm with the remaining wrapped around the hands. The following blessing is said before donning the *shel rosh t'fillin*:

> *Barukh atah Adonai, eloheynu melekh ha' olam, asher kidshanu b' mitzvotav v' tzivanu al mitzvat t'fillin.*

Blessed art Thou, O Lord our God, King of the universe, who has sanctified us by His commandments and commanded us concerning the command of t'fillin.

The *shel rosh t'fillin* is placed upon the head with the straps secured and the remaining length draped over the chest. This additional blessing is recited:

> *Barukh sheym k'vod malkhuto l'olam va'ed.*

Blessed be His Name whose glorious kingdom is forever and ever.

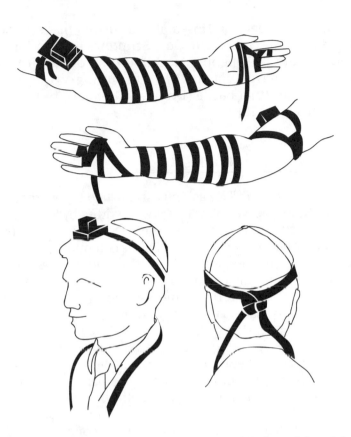

The final step is to tie the remaining leather of the *shel yad* *t'fillin* around the fingers in the symbolic knots. It is wound three times around the middle finger, with one loop around the middle part of the finger and two loops closer to the knuckle. The strap is then wrapped around the ring finger while the following Scripture is recited:

> I will betroth you to me forever; I will betroth you in righteousness and justice, in love and compassion. I will betroth you in faithfulness, and you will acknowledge the LORD (Hosea 2:19–20).

It is unfortunate that some people may become lost in all the knots and miss the beauty of what *t'fillin* represents. As seen from the verses in Hosea, it is a custom that signifies Israel's marriage covenant to God. Scriptures are to be in the minds of all God's people, and upon the deeds of their hands. Some have compared t'fillin to putting on the armor of God for spiritual battle (Donin, To Be a Jew, p. 151; cf., Ephesians 6:10–20).

RELEVANCE TO THE NEW TESTAMENT

The custom of t'fillin was well established before the first century. Since the New Testament was written by Jews about Jewish topics, one would expect there to be mention of this very traditional element of the religious community. There is actually only one mention of t'fillin (Greek phylacteries) in the New Testament, which is found in the words of Yeshua.

As he was exposing the corruption and hypocrisy of some of the religious leaders of his day, Yeshua said:

They tie heavy loads onto people's shoulders but won't lift a finger to help carry them. Everything they do is done to be seen by others; for they make their t'fillin broad and their tzitziyot [fringes] long (Matthew 23:4–5).

The fact that Yeshua was not outright condemning the use of t'fillin or tzitziyot has been shown in the previous chapter on the fringes. Since Yeshua certainly wore the tzitziyot himself (see Matthew 9:20), he was speaking only against the abuse of this God-given custom. The same can be implied concerning the use of t'fillin. If Yeshua perfectly kept the Law, one can assume that he would have followed this Jewish custom as well. However, when man-made confusion was added to the customs of God, the Messiah stepped in with the proper rebuke.

It is significant to note that the Talmud also agrees that this over-emphasis on externals did indeed creep into many of the biblical customs. In regard to t'fillin, the rabbis recount how some people enlarged the leather boxes to fulfill the verse that "all the peoples of the earth shall see that the name of the Lord is called upon thee" (Deuteronomy 28:10, as quoted in *Babylonian Talmud*, Berachot 6a). It is very unfortunate, yet very human, for people to take a custom that was meant to keep their mind focused on the Lord and focus on self instead. It seems that Yeshua was fulfilling part of the mission of Messiah—to call the Jewish people back to the true spiritual intention of the Torah.

There is another important reference in the New Testament that reminds one of the symbolism behind the *t'fillin*. In the Book of Revelation, *Yokhanan* had a prophetic vision that revealed many details regarding the second coming of Messiah Yeshua. He wrote concerning the coming false prophet:

> Also it [the false prophet] forces everyone—great and small, rich and poor, free and slave—to receive a mark on his right hand or on his forehead preventing anyone from buying or selling unless he has the mark, that is, the name of the beast or the number of its name. This is where wisdom is needed; those who understand should count the number of the beast, for it is the number of a person, and its number is 666 (Revelation 13:16–18).

The message is clearer for a reader who understands the biblical/Jewish customs. By following the command to wear the *t'fillin*, the Jew is reminded that his mind (forehead) and his actions (hand) are to be dedicated to the glory of God. It is no coincidence that when the false Messiah comes, he will try to usurp that same symbolism for his own deceptive reasons. Instead of the name of God (*Shaddai*, "Almighty") displayed by means of the *t'fillin*, the world will be required to wear the name of the false Messiah ("666") in order to purchase any goods.

The spiritual lessons taught by a proper use of *t'fillin* are rich and deep. While the New Testament often alludes to various customs and traditions, invariably it draws one back to spiritual reality. The minds of believers in Yeshua are to be protected by the Word of God as their hands are to do the will of God. The Greek word *phylacteries* is often translated "to guard or protect," which is consistent with the spiritual purposes of *t'fillin*. As Saul of Tarsus summarized:

And this is why I suffer as I do. But I am not ashamed, because I know in whom I have put my trust, and I am persuaded that he can keep safe until that Day what he has entrusted to me (2 Timothy 1:12).

God has promised to guard the hearts and lives of believers as they walk with him. May every believer walk in the spiritual realities secured through the custom of *t'fillin*.

PRACTICAL GUIDE FOR THE MESSIANIC USE OF T'FILLIN

The custom of *t'fillin* is biblically based as well as spiritually rich. Messianic Jews and like-minded Gentiles may choose to wear *t'fillin* if they feel that it would be a blessing to their spiritual life. The details of how to "lay *t'fillin*" (as it is called) need not be changed substantially for a Messianic believer. While believers are not bound by the innumerable rabbinic details, many of the ancient customs make sense for Bible-believers as well. Believers can use their liberty in Messiah to make their understanding of this ancient tradition more meaningful. Whatever the expression is, may every believer always fulfill the intent of the *t'fillin* by having their minds and hands serving Messiah.

Conclusion

The Blessing of the Customs

It is my hope that this book has been an informative study, providing material to develop a new appreciation for the biblical/Jewish customs. God appointed these customs to bless his people, both Jews and Gentiles. All believers in Yeshua can benefit spiritually by understanding God's purpose behind each of these *traditions*. Whatever one's lifestyle in the Lord, may every believer be blessed by gaining a fresh appreciation for God's appointed customs.

If you are interested in understanding and/or observing God's appointed customs, nearly all of the books, products, and other items can be obtained from Jewish bookstores or from Messianic Jewish Resources International, a division of The Lederer Foundation. Call (800) 410-7367 to receive a free Messianic Jewish Resources catalog or to order products. Or shop via the Internet at http://www.MessianicJewish.net.

Glossary

adam	man
adamah	dust, earth
Adonai Ekhad	The LORD is One
aliyot	goings up
amidah	18 benedictions
b'rachah	blessing
b'ris	covenant (Ashkenazi pronunciation)
b'rit	covenant (Sephardic pronunciation)
b'rit milah	covenant of circumcision
baptidzo	a Greek word meaning to totally immerse
bar	son
Bar/Bat Mitzvah	Son/Daughter of the Commandment
barukh habah b'shem Adonai	blessed is he who comes in the name of the LORD
bat	daughter
bayit	house
ben	son
beyt	house

Beyt Ha'Mikdash	Holy Temple
bimah	pulpit, platform
birkat ha'mazon	blessing over the meal
challah	sabbath bread
Cohanim	Priests, the sons of Aaron
drashah	sermon, teaching
eyrusin	betrothal
fleishig	meat products
Gemara	commentary on the Mishnah
get	divorce decree
Geyhinnom	Hell
Haftarah	section read from the Prophets
halakhah	traditional law
huppah	canopy
kashrut	dietary laws
kesher	knot
ketubah	marriage contract
kiddush	sanctification, often a cup of wine to "set apart" an event
kiddushin	the betrothal ceremony
kippah, -ot	skullcap(s)
kisey shel Eliyahu	chair of Elijah
kosher	fit for consumption, clean
kvatter	godfather
kvatterin	godmother
Levi'im	sons of the tribe of Levi
m'zuzah, -ot	doorpost(s), a small box containing two handwritten biblical passages (Deut 6:4–9 and Deut. 11:13–21) on parchment; the box is attached to the doors of people's homes
maftir	the person who reads the Haftarah and the concluding section of the Torah portion; therefore, the concluding section of the Torah portion
masoret	that which is handed down from past generations
mazel tov	congratulations

mevoreykh	one who blesses
midrash	rabbinical commentary on the *Torah*
mikisey l'yad ha'av	from the chair to the hand of the father
mikveh, -ot	special pool(s) constructed for ritual water immersion
milchiy	dairy products
Miryam	Miriam, Mary
Mishnah	the Oral Law in written form, a codification (topical) based on the *Torah* (the Written Law)
mitznefet	a miter or a turban-style of headcovering
mitzvah	commandment
mohel	person who performs religious circumcisions
Moshe ben Maimon	Maimonides
n'veylah	meat from animals that have not been slaughtered, a carcass
Natzeret	Nazareth
niddah	removed, separated
nissuin	marriage
oneg	joyful celebration
oy vey	Oh my!
paradosis	a Greek word that means that which is handed down from past generations
parve	neutral, neither meat nor dairy food
pidyon ha'ben	redemption of the firstborn
Rosh Hashanah	Jewish New Year, head of the year
Ruakh HaKodesh	Holy Spirit
sandek	person who holds the baby during circumcision
sandek sheni	second Sandek
seder	order (Passover meal)
seudah mitzvah	meal of the commandment

sh'khitah	ritual slaughtering procedure
Sh'ma	refers to Deuteronomy 6:4–6; Hear (oh Israel)
shabbat	sabbath
Shaddai	Almighty
shadkhan	marriage broker, matchmaker
shakharit	daily morning services
shaliakh	representative
Shavuot	Pentecost, Feast of Weeks
shel rosh	head t'fillin, designated for the head
shel yad	hand t'fillin, designated for the hand
sheva b'rakhot	seven blessings
shiddukhin	arrangements preliminary to betrothal
Shim'on	Simeon, Simon
Shim'on Kefa	Simon Peter
Shlomo ben Yitzkhak	Rashi (famous rabbinic commentator)
shofar	ram's horn
shokhet	kosher butcher
Shomeyr daltot Yisraeyl	Watchman of the doors of Israel
siddur, -im	prayer book(s)
simcha	joyous occasion
t'fillah	prayer
t'fillin	phylacteries, leather boxes strapped to the forehead and hand
t'kheylet	blue dye extracted from a Mediterranean sea snail, used for the blue thread in the prayer shawl
t'reyfah	food that comes from animals killed by wild beasts
t'vilah	to totally immerse
tahor	clean, kosher
tallis	prayer shawl
tallit katan	small prayer shawl

tallit, -ot	prayer shawl(s)
Talmud	codified body of rabbinic thought; Mishnah plus Gemara
tamey	unclean
tareyf	unclean food
tashlikh	ceremony of repentance that takes place at a body of water
tzilzil, -yot	fringe(s) worn on a garment
yarmulke	Yiddish word meaning headcovering
yeshu'ah	salvation
Yeshua	Jesus, salvation
Yeshua HaMashiakh	Jesus the Messiah
Yokhanan	John
Yom Kippur	Day of Atonement
Yosef	Joseph
Z'kharyah	Zechariah

Bibliography

Birnbaum, Philip. *A Book of Jewish Concepts*. New York: Hebrew Publishing Company, 1975.

————, ed. *Maimonides Code of Law and Ethics: Mishneh Torah*. New York: Hebrew Publishing Company, 1974.

Buxbaum, Yitzhak. *Jewish Spiritual Practices*. Northvale: N.J. Jason Aronson Inc., 1994.

Central Conference of American Rabbis. *Rabbi's Manual*. Philadelphia: Maurice Jacobs, Inc., 1961.

Cohen, A. *The Five Megilloth*. New York: Soncino Press, 1983.

Cohn, Haim. *The Trial and Death of Jesus*. New York: Ktav Publishing House, 1977.

Connolly, Peter. *Living in the Time of Jesus of Nazareth*. Tel Aviv: Steimatzky Ltd., 1988.

157

Davies, W.D. *Paul and Rabbinic Judaism*. Philadelphia: Fortress Press, 1980.

Donin, Hayim Halevy. *To Be a Jew*. New York: Basic Books, 1972.

Edersheim, Alfred. *The Life and Times of Jesus the Messiah*. Grand Rapids: Eerdmans Publishing, 1984.

————. *Sketches of Jewish Social Life in the Days of Christ*. Grand Rapids: Eerdmans Publishing, 1978.

Encyclopedia Judaica. Jerusalem: Keter Publishing House, 1972.

Epstein, Isidore, ed. *Hebrew-English Edition of the Babylonian Talmud*. London: The Soncino Press, 1960.

Fischer, John. *Messianic Services for the Festivals & Holy Days*. Palm Harbor, Fla.: Menorah Ministries, 1992.

Fischer, John, and David Bronstein. *Siddur for Messianic Jews*. Palm Harbor, Fla.: Menorah Ministries, 1988.

Flusser, David. *Jewish Sources in Early Christianity*. Tel Aviv: MOD Books, 1989.

Freedman, H., and Maurice Simon. *The Midrash Rabbah: Exodus Rabbah*. London: The Soncino Press, 1977.

Fruchtenbaum, Arnold. *Hebrew Christianity: Its Theology, History and Philosophy*. San Antonio: Ariel Press, 1983.

————. *Israelology: The Missing Link in Systematic Theology*. Tustin, Calif.: Ariel Ministries Press, 1993.

Goldberg, Louis. *Our Jewish Friends*. Neptune, N.J.: Loizeaux Brothers, 1984.

Gower, Ralph. *The New Manners and Customs of Bible Times*. Chicago: Moody, 1987.

Greenberg, Jeremiah. *Messianic Wedding Ceremony.* Tape. Odessa, Fla.: Messianic Liturgical Resources, 1995.

Hilton, Michael, and Gordian Marshall. *The Gospels & Rabbinic Judaism.* Hoboken, N.J.: Ktav Publishing House, 1988.

Juster, Daniel. *Jewish Roots.* Gaithersburg, Md.: Davar, 1986.

Kasdan, Barney. *God's Appointed Times.* Baltimore: Lederer Messianic Publications, 1993.

Kesher—A Journal on Messianic Judaism 1 (July 1994).

Klausner, Joseph. *Jesus of Nazareth.* New York: Menorah Pub-lishing Company, 1979.

Klein, Isaac. *A Guide to Jewish Religious Practice.* New York: The Jewish Theological Seminary Of America, 1979.

Lachs, Samuel Tobias. *A Rabbinic Commentary on the New Testament.* Hoboken, N.J.: Ktav Publishing House, 1987.

Lamm, Maurice. *The Jewish Way in Death and Mourning.* New York: Jonathan David Publishers, 1969.

Lash, Neil and Jamie. *The Jewish Wedding.* Tape. Fort Lauderdale: Love Song to the Messiah, 1990.

Neusner, Jacob, ed. *The Talmud of the Land of Israel* [Jerusalem Talmud]. Chicago: The University of Chicago Press, 1982.

Olitzky, Kerry and Ronald Isaacs. *The How to Handbook for Jewish Living.* Hoboken, N.J.: Ktav, 1993.

————. *The Second How to Handbook for Jewish Living.* Hoboken, N.J.: Ktav, 1996.

Patai, Raphael. *The Messiah Texts.* New York: Avon Books, 1979.

Philips, A.T. *Daily Prayers*. New York: Hebrew Publishing Company.

Robertson, A.T. *Word Pictures in the New Testament*. Grand Rapids: Baker Book House, 1931.

Rosten, Leo. *The Joys of Yiddish*. New York: Pocket Books, 1977.

Rubin, Barry. *You Bring the Bagels; I'll Bring the Gospel*. Old Tappan, N.J.: Chosen Books, 1989.

Scherman, Nosson. *The Rabbinical Council of America Edition of The Artscroll Siddur*. NY: Mesorah Publications, Ltd., 1990.

Siegel, Richard, and Michael and Sharon Strassfeld. *The First Jewish Catalog*. Philadelphia: The Jewish Publication Society.

Silverman, Morris. *Sabbath and Festival Prayer Book*. USA: United Synagogue Of America, 1979.

Stern, David. *Jewish New Testament Commentary*. Clarksville, Md.: Jewish New Testament Publications, 1992.

————. *Messianic Jewish Manifesto*. Clarksville, Md.: Jewish New Testament Publications, 1988.

Whiston, William. *Josephus' Complete Works*. Grand Rapids: Kregel Publications, 1960.

Wouk, Herman. *This Is My God*. New York: Simon & Schuster, 1986.